WHILE THE SUN SHINES

WHILE THE SUN SHINES

a comedy

by

TERENCE RATTIGAN

Author of

FRENCH WITHOUT TEARS
AFTER THE DANCE
FIRST EPISODE
FLARE PATH

HAMISH HAMILTON
LONDON

FIRST PUBLISHED 1944

To

ANTHONY ASQUITH

MADE AND PRINTED IN GREAT BRITAIN
BY THE STANHOPE PRESS LIMITED
ROCHESTER   :   KENT

CHARACTERS

HORTON

THE EARL OF HARPENDEN

LIEUTENANT MULVANEY

LADY ELISABETH RANDALL

THE DUKE OF AYR AND STIRLING

LIEUTENANT COLBERT

MABEL CRUM

*The action passes in the sitting-room of
Lord Harpenden's chambers in Albany, London.*

ACT I
Morning.

ACT II
Night.

ACT III
SCENE I. *Late night.*
SCENE II. *Morning.*

WHILE THE SUN SHINES

was first produced at the Globe Theatre, London, on
December 24, 1943, with the following cast:

HORTON	*Douglas Jeffries*
THE EARL OF HARPENDEN . .	*Michael Wilding*
LIEUTENANT MULVANEY . . .	*Hugh McDermott*
LADY ELISABETH RANDALL . . .	*Jane Baxter*
THE DUKE OF AYR AND STIRLING .	*Ronald Squire*
LIEUTENANT COLBERT . . .	*Eugene Deckers*
MABEL CRUM	*Brenda Bruce*

The play directed by *Anthony Asquith*

NOTE

ACT I

SCENE: *The sitting-room of Lord Harpenden's chambers in Albany, London. A large, square room, furnished solidly with late eighteenth-century mahogany furniture. Double doors back centre lead into the bedroom; a single door, L., into the hall. Large windows take up most of the right wall.*

HORTON, *Lord Harpenden's manservant, comes in. He is carrying a breakfast tray, which he puts down on a table. He is a thin, gloomy-faced man of about fifty. He knocks gently on the bedroom door. Receiving no reply, he opens the door and goes in—to emerge instantly. He closes the door again, ponders a second, and then knocks loudly. There is still no answer. He knocks again.* LORD HARPENDEN *comes out, looking tousled and sleepy. He is a young man of twenty-three or twenty-four, of rather frail appearance.*

HARPENDEN. What's the matter?

HORTON. Your breakfast is ready, my Lord.

HARPENDEN. Yes. So I see—but why did you dart in and out like that, like a scared rabbit?

HORTON. I—beg your pardon, my Lord.

HARPENDEN *surveys his appearance in a wall mirror, and gives a faint shudder of disgust. He begins to comb his hair with a small pocket-comb.*

HARPENDEN. Oh, Horton, bring another breakfast, will you?

HORTON. Yes, my Lord.

HARPENDEN. What have you got?

HORTON. Well, there's some spam.

HARPENDEN. No, don't waste the spam; it's too useful for sandwiches, late at night. What about sausages?

HORTON. I can manage one, my Lord.

HARPENDEN. That'll do.

HORTON. It's tea and not coffee, isn't it, my Lord?

HARPENDEN. What do you mean? (*He has picked up the* Times *and is glancing through it.*)

1

HORTON.   Miss Crum prefers tea to coffee for breakfast.

HARPENDEN.   Miss Crum? Who said anything about Miss Crum?

HORTON.   Isn't it Miss Crum?

HARPENDEN.   No, it is not Miss Crum.

HORTON. (*doubtfully*).   It looked like Miss Crum.

HARPENDEN (*raising his voice*).   I don't care who it looked like—it is not Miss Crum. As a matter of fact it isn't Miss Anything——

HORTON. Mrs. Chappel?

HARPENDEN.   Horton—you haven't by any chance forgotten that I'm getting married tomorrow?

HORTON.   No, my Lord.

HARPENDEN.   Very well, then. Now, will you kindly go into that room, draw the curtains, take a good look around, and then come out and tell me how sorry you are.

HORTON.   I hardly like to do that, my Lord.

HARPENDEN.   Go on.

(HORTON *goes into the bedroom. There comes the sound of curtains being drawn, then* HORTON *reappears and closes the door.*)

HORTON.   I'm extremely sorry, my Lord.

HARPENDEN.   Thank you, Horton.

HORTON.   Funny, it looked just like Miss Crum, the way she sleeps all curled up with her arm over her face——

(*He is interrupted by a wail from* HARPENDEN, *who has taken the cover off his breakfast dish.*)

HARPENDEN.   Horton—what's happened to my grandmother's other egg?

HORTON.   Well, my Lord——

HARPENDEN.   There were two—you know there were. She sent me two, and I had one yesterday—now where's the other?

(*There is a slight pause before* HORTON *can gain enough courage to answer.*)

HORTON.   There was an accident, my Lord.

HARPENDEN.   Oh, no!

HORTON.   I'm afraid so, my Lord.

HARPENDEN (*with a wealth of reproach*). Oh, Horton!

HORTON. I had taken the egg out of the refrigerator, and I was just going to break it on the side of the frying-pan when——

HARPENDEN. Please, Horton, this is too painful. I'd rather not hear anything more about it.

HORTON. No. my Lord. I'm very sorry.

(*The telephone rings.* HORTON *goes to answer it.*)

Hullo . . . Yes, m'lady. (*He puts the receiver down.*) Lady Elisabeth.

(HARPENDEN *gets up and takes the receiver.* HORTON *goes out.*)

HARPENDEN. Hullo, darling. How are you? Have a good journey? . . . Not the whole night? . . . Couldn't you get a sleeper? . . . Well, surely your father could have fixed it for you . . . through the Air Ministry. . . . Yes, but I consider coming up to marry me is work of national importance . . . How are you? . . Yes, I know, but apart from that, how are you? . . . Good. You didn't have any trouble about leave? . . . When? . . . Wednesday? . . . Well, that gives us six days . . .

(MULVANEY, *a young American in the late twenties, appears at the bedroom door. He has swathed an eiderdown round his otherwise naked body.*)

(*To* MULVANEY) Good-morning.

MULVANEY. Good-morning. (*He looks round the room, blinking in the daylight.*)

HARPENDEN (*into telephone*). No, darling, nobody you know . . .

Well, not this morning, darling, because I've got an interview at the Admiralty. Let's meet for lunch. One o'clock at Pruniers. All right? Where are you staying? Brown's? . . . How did you get in? . . . Three weeks ago? . . . No, I had a very quiet evening, in bed at ten . . . All right, don't believe it . . . it's true . . . See you at lunch then . . . Goodbye. (*He replaces the receiver. To* MULVANEY) Let me get you a dressing-gown.

(*He goes into the bedroom.* MULVANEY *continues his*

bewildered scrutiny of the room. HARPENDEN *comes out with a dressing-gown, which he gives to* MULVANEY, *who nods his thanks.*)

MULVANEY. Pardon me—where am I?

HARPENDEN. You're in my chambers in Albany.

MULVANEY. What are chambers?

HARPENDEN. Flat. Apartment.

MULVANEY. What's Albany?

HARPENDEN. It's a sort of block of chambers—apartments —off Piccadilly.

MULVANEY. And, if you'll pardon me again, who are you?

HARPENDEN. My name's Harpenden.

MULVANEY. Mine's Mulvaney. Glad to know you.

(*They shake hands.*)

HARPENDEN. How do you do. Do you mind if I start my breakfast? Yours is on the way.

MULVANEY. Go right ahead. Was that your bed I slept in?

(HARPENDEN *sits down to his breakfast.*)

HARPENDEN. Yes.

MULVANEY. Oh. Have I been there since ten, last night?

HARPENDEN. What? Oh, no. You see, I didn't see any point in volunteering the information to one's strictly brought up fiancée that one spent half the night in the Jubilee.

MULVANEY. The Jubilee? Now, that name seems to pull a plug. Was I there last night?

HARPENDEN. Well—you looked in——

MULVANEY (*nodding*). And looked out?

HARPENDEN. Shall we say your exit was more involuntary than your entrance?

MULVANEY. It's coming back to me. They gave me the bum's rush, didn't they?

HARPENDEN. You could put it that way, I suppose. I didn't really see it. One minute you were there, doing a pas seul in the centre of the floor, and the next minute you were in the street.

MULVANEY. What's a pas seul?

HARPENDEN. A little dance on your own.

MULVANEY. Was that what I was doing?

HARPENDEN. That is the charitable view of what you were doing.

MULVANEY. What's the uncharitable view?

HARPENDEN. Pinching Mrs. Warner's behind.

MULVANEY. Who's Mrs. Warner?

HARPENDEN. The proprietress of the Jubilee.

MULVANEY. Oh, my aching back! So I'm in the street. What happens then?

HARPENDEN. Well, when I left the place, about half an hour later, I tripped over you in the black-out.

MULVANEY. Gee, was I lying there unconscious all that time?

HARPENDEN. Semi-conscious.

MULVANEY. Knocked out, huh?

HARPENDEN. No. Passed out.

MULVANEY. Say, listen — how could you tell the difference?

HARPENDEN. I'd rather not go into that at the moment.

MULVANEY. O.K. O.K. Only let me tell you, concussion can take some funny forms.

HARPENDEN. I doubt if concussion would take the form of breathing gin fumes in my face and calling me Dulcie.

MULVANEY. Did I call you Dulcie?

HARPENDEN. Amongst other things.

MULVANEY. Gosh! How did I come to do that, I wonder?

HARPENDEN. Not knowing Dulcie, it's hard for me to say.

MULVANEY. She's my girl friend back home.

HARPENDEN. So I gathered.

MULVANEY. You don't look a bit like her.

HARPENDEN. That's too bad.

MULVANEY. Well, go on. What happened then?

HARPENDEN. You wouldn't tell me where you lived. At least you gave your address as 856 Orinoco Avenue, Elizabeth City, Ohio.

MULVANEY. Yeah, That's where I live all right.

HARPENDEN. Yes, but it didn't help the immediate problem of finding you a bed.

MULVANEY. You could have taken me to the Jules Club or somewhere.

HARPENDEN. I thought of that, but not knowing the customs of the American Army I wasn't sure how they would view the parking on their doorstep at four o'clock in the morning of a very pickled lieutenant, inclined to embrace everyone he saw and call them Dulcie.

MULVANEY (*after a moment's thought*). It would have been O.K.

HARPENDEN. I didn't like to risk a court-martial.

MULVANEY. So you brought me here.

HARPENDEN. The porter and I carried you up and put you to bed.

MULVANEY. Say, I hope I didn't disgrace you.

HARPENDEN. Oh, that's quite all right. The porters here have been used to putting people to bed for well over a hundred years. Lord Byron had chambers in Albany.

MULVANEY (*interested*). Did he now? Say, isn't that something? It is kind of old world, this place, at that.

HARPENDEN. Yes, it is. I like it very much. My family have always lived here.

MULVANEY. Do they live here now?

HARPENDEN. No, I haven't any family—at least, I'm an orphan.

MULVANEY. Tough. Gee, it gives one quite a kick to have slept in a place Byron used to sleep in. Did he write any of his poetry here, do you think?

HARPENDEN. I expect so.

MULVANEY (*quoting*).

> So we'll go no more a-roving
> So late into the night,
> Though the heart . . . (*falters*).

How does it go on?

HARPENDEN. I'm afraid I don't know. I don't read Byron.

MULVANEY (*remembering*).

> Though the heart be still as loving
> And the moon be still as bright.

Imagine your not reading Byron.

HARPENDEN. Imagine.

MULVANEY. That's funny, you know.

HARPENDEN (*piqued*). I don't see why it's funny—quite a lot of people don't read Byron.

MULVANEY. Yeah. But—hell—you live here.

(HORTON *comes in with another breakfast tray.*)

HARPENDEN. Here's your breakfast.

MULVANEY (*to* HORTON). Take it away, Buddy. I couldn't use it.

(HORTON *looks at* HARPENDEN *in doubt.*)

HARPENDEN. You'd better try and eat something. It's supposed to be good for—er—for concussion.

MULVANEY. O.K. I'll try a cup of coffee.

(HORTON *begins to pour out a cup of coffee.*)

Gee, I almost forgot to thank you for being my good Samaritan.

HARPENDEN. Oh, that's all right. I hope you'll do the same for me one day.

MULVANEY. You bet, in the event you ever come to Elizabeth City and get yourself thrown out of Smokey Joe's.

HARPENDEN. All right, Horton. You can clear this away now (*he indicates his tray*).

HORTON. Very good, my Lord.

(MULVANEY *starts, looks at* HORTON *and then at* HARPENDEN, *as if at a strange animal.*)

HARPENDEN. You're in the Air Corps, aren't you?

MULVANEY (*still staring at* HARPENDEN). That's right.

HARPENDEN. Pilot?

MULVANEY. Bombardier.

HARPENDEN. Liberators?

MULVANEY. Forts.

(*He continues to scrutinise* HARPENDEN, *who becomes conscious of his gaze and looks uncomfortable.* HORTON, *meanwhile, has collected* HARPENDEN'S *breakfast tray.*)

HORTON.   Will you be wearing your uniform, my Lord?

HARPENDEN.   Yes.   My best one.   I'm going to the Admiralty.

(MULVANEY *puts his coffee cup down with a clatter.*)

MULVANEY (*to* HORTON).   You wouldn't fool me, would you?

HORTON.   No, sir.

MULVANEY (*to* HARPENDEN).   Are you a lord?

HARPENDEN.   Er—yes——

MULVANEY.   You said your name was Harpenden.

HARPENDEN.   That's right.

MULVANEY.   You mean you're Lord Harpenden?

HORTON.   The Earl of Harpenden.

(HORTON *goes out.*)

MULVANEY.   So you're an earl?

HARPENDEN.   Er—yes—I'm afraid so!

(*There is a pause while* MULVANEY *gazes at* HARPENDEN *intently.*)

You're the first earl I ever saw.

HARPENDEN.   Oh, they're quite common, really, you know——

MULVANEY.   It's funny.   You seemed quite an ordinary sort of guy.

HARPENDEN.   I am quite an ordinary sort of guy.

MULVANEY.   Don't give me that.   You're an earl.   Say, listen, what do I call you?

HARPENDEN.   My friends usually call me Bobby.

MULVANEY.   I wouldn't call you that.

HARPENDEN.   Why not?

MULVANEY.   It doesn't seem right.

HARPENDEN.   Last night you called me Dulcie.

MULVANEY (*ashamed*).   Gosh!   So I did.

HARPENDEN.   What's your Christian name?

MULVANEY.   Joe.

HARPENDEN.   Right.   It's Joe and Bobby from now on. Now listen—I've got to go and dress.   How long is your leave?

MULVANEY.   Seven days.

HARPENDEN. Where are you staying in London?

MULVANEY. Nowhere yet. I only got up yesterday.

HARPENDEN. Well, you can stay here if you like.

MULVANEY. Hell, no—I couldn't do that.

HARPENDEN. That's all right. I won't be here after tomorrow. I'm getting married, you see, and we're spending our leave together in Oxford.

MULVANEY. Gee—congratulations!

HARPENDEN. Thanks, Joe.

MULVANEY. What's that going to make her? I mean, what's the feminine of earl?

HARPENDEN. Countess.

MULVANEY (disappointed). Oh, Countess. I knew a girl became a Countess. She married an Italian.

HARPENDEN. Really?

MULVANEY. She got herself a divorce, and now she's back in Elizabeth City, but she's still a Countess.

HARPENDEN. Well, of course, Italian Countesses don't mean very much—I don't mean to be rude to your friend.

MULVANEY. That's O.K.—Elly's a good girl, but she's not one of Nature's Countesses.

HARPENDEN. So much for Elly. Well, now, it's settled, isn't it? You're going to stay here for your leave?

MULVANEY. Well, it's darned kind of you, Bobby.

HARPENDEN. My man, Horton, will look after you.

MULVANEY (giggling). Your man, Horton. Gee, this slays me!

(HARPENDEN smiles politely.)

HARPENDEN. Well, I must go and dress.

MULVANEY. Just a minute. Before I finally accept your very kind invitation, would it be all right to—well, you know, a guy might feel kind of lonely at times, and——

HARPENDEN. Yes, that's all right. Horton's very discreet.

MULVANEY. It's a kind of hypothetical question, anyway. I don't know a darned soul in this town.

HARPENDEN. Don't you? Oh, well, we'll soon fix that. What's your type—anything special?

MULVANEY. Under fifty.

(HARPENDEN *has begun to dial a number.*)

HARPENDEN. I'm ringing up someone who's very good-looking, very amusing, and mad about Americans. (*Into receiver*) Hullo. Extension 5651 please. Thanks. (*To* MULVANEY) She works at the Air Ministry . . . Typist . . .

MULVANEY. A what?

HARPENDEN. Typist. Stenographer, you know.

MULVANEY. Oh . . .

HARPENDEN (*into receiver*). Hullo. Could I speak to Miss Crum, please? Lord Harpenden . . . (*To* MULVANEY) I'll ask her round for a drink and then you could invite her to dinner or something . . . (*into receiver*) Hullo, Mabel . . . Bobby . . . How are you? . . . Well, I've told you before not to go out with Poles . . . Yes, I know they're pets, but that's not the point . . . Look, darling, what time is that horrible old Sir Archibald letting you off today? . . . Well, what are you doing at the office if it's your day off? . . . Oh, I see. What about coming round here for a drink? . . . Albany . . . In about an hour . . . There's an American I want you to meet . . . yes, a pet . . . he's a Bombardier . . . he's got the most wonderful story about a raid on Bremen that'll thrill you to the marrow . . . All right, darling . . . I may be out, but he'll be here anyway . . . Yes, I'll try to be in, but I've got an interview at the Admiralty . . . I don't suppose it'll take long . . . That's the girl . . . yes, tomorrow . . . St. George's, Hanover Square. You're coming, aren't you? . . . Yes, you did. You met her at a cocktail party, about a year ago . . . Yes, that's right. Brown hair and grey eyes . . . Darling, you are speaking of the woman I love . . . Yes, I do, really I do . . . Yes, of course I love you too, but in a different way . . . All right. Bless you.

(*He rings off.*)

She's coming round this morning. She's got the day off, so you can ask her to lunch.

MULVANEY. I've never done a raid on Bremen.

HARPENDEN (*vaguely*). Haven't you? Oh well, I don't suppose she'll mind.

MULVANEY. Say, this is darned kind of you.

HARPENDEN. Oh, that's all right. Just look on it as a bit of reciprocal lease-lend.

(*He goes into the bedroom.*)

MULVANEY (*calling*). Say, Bobby—can I use your phone?

HARPENDEN (*off*). Yes—of course.

(MULVANEY *goes to the telephone. He dials a number.*)

MULVANEY. Hullo. Can I speak to Colonel Murphy, please? Lieutenant Mulvaney . . .

(HORTON *comes in and crosses the room to the bedroom door.*)

HORTON (*at door*). Was your breakfast to your liking, sir?

MULVANEY (*with an air of dignity*). Yes, thank you, Horton.

(*He giggles suddenly.* HORTON *raises his eyebrows and goes into the bedroom.*)

(*Into receiver*) Hullo, Spike? . . . Say, listen, what happened to you guys last night? . . . Yeah, I remember as far as that, but how come I got to a joint called the Jubilee all by myself? . . . Oh, what was she like? . . . O.K., I'll tell you, but you won't believe me. I slept in the same bed with an earl . . . No, not a girl, stupid, an earl. E-A-R-L. An earl . . . Hell, no, I wouldn't kid you, Spike. (*Angrily*) Because he says he's an earl . . . Well, you got to believe a guy when he says a thing like that . . .

(HORTON *comes out of the bedroom, with* MULVANEY'S *uniform over his arm.*)

No, they don't wear crowns. Only when they go to Westminster Abbey—I know that—(*He catches sight of* HORTON) Hey, where are you going with my uniform?

HORTON. I was going to brush it, sir. If I may say so, it needs a good brushing badly.

MULVANEY. Righty-oh, old fellow. (*He giggles again.*)

(HORTON *goes out.*)

MULVANEY (*into receiver*). That was his man, Horton. Doesn't it slay you? . . . The earl? Well, he's young—younger than me . . . You can, too, be an earl when you're young. Remember little Lord Fauntleroy . . . Well, the

little Duke, then . . . you're a disbelieving son of a bitch
. . . A place called the Albany . . . Sort of old-fashioned
apartment house, only the apartments are called chambers
. . . Wise guy . . . Yeah, Lord Byron lived here . . .
Lord Byron . . . No, he's dead, you ignorant bastard.
Don't you know anything except how to drive a B.17? . . .
(HORTON *comes in*.)

This guy's called Harpenden—the Earl of Harpenden . . .
Not a bad little guy. (*He catches sight of* HORTON) A crack-
ing good sort . . . See you tonight at the Club . . . O.K.
Goodbye. (*He rings off*.)

HORTON.   Excuse me, sir, did you want your buttons
cleaned?

MULVANEY.   Er—no thanks. We don't clean our buttons.

HORTON.   Very good, sir. (*He turns to go*.)

MULVANEY.   Say, don't go for a minute. Stay and talk.

HORTON.   Sir?

MULVANEY.   How long have you been the earl's man?

HORTON.   I've been with his Lordship all his life. Before
that I was with his father.

MULVANEY.   You're not the only man he's got, I suppose?

HORTON.   No, sir. We have two large country estates, and
before the war they needed a very big staff to keep them up.

MULVANEY.   Before the war? What's happened to them
now?

HORTON.   One is a hospital, and the other has been taken
over by the Air Force.

MULVANEY.   That's tough.

HORTON.   Tough, sir?

MULVANEY.   Well, I've read a lot about how these English
aristocrats are being ruined by the war——

HORTON.   Oh, no, sir. We are far from being ruined.
Luckily our money doesn't come from our estates, which
were always run at a loss, even before the war.

MULVANEY.   What does it come from, then?

HORTON.   Ground rents, sir—in London, mostly.

MULVANEY.   Real estate, huh? That's pretty valuable,
I guess——

HORTON. Yes, sir. We must be worth all of two million pounds, sir.

MULVANEY. Holy smoke! Eight million dollars!

HORTON. Yes, sir, Probably a good deal more than that.

MULVANEY. Gee!

(*He ponders for a second.* HORTON *waits patiently for his next question.*)

You know, it doesn't seem right to me that a guy should be worth all that money and not to have had to work for it.

HORTON. It happens in your country, too, sir.

MULVANEY. Yeah, I suppose it does. Still, we don't call them earls.

HORTON. No, sir.

MULVANEY. You mustn't mind me. I'm just an ignorant American.

HORTON. I'm an American myself, sir. I was born in America and had an American father.

MULVANEY. Is that so?

HORTON. My mother went to New York before I was born. She was a housemaid with the Morgan family there. She married an American opera singer.

MULVANEY. She did? Well, how come you're not at the Metropolitan yourself?

HORTON. I fancy I inherited my mother's talents rather than my father's. Anyway, I understand he was not a very good opera singer. Well, now, sir, if you'll excuse me, I'd better be getting on with my work.

MULVANEY. Sure thing. Sorry to have kept you.

HORTON. Not at all, sir. Very glad to have a chat with a fellow citizen.

(*He goes out. Left alone,* MULVANEY *looks around the room with a new expression on his face.*)

MULVANEY (*muttering to himself*). Eight million bucks!

(HARPENDEN *comes out of the bedroom. He is dressed as an ordinary seaman, less boots.* MULVANEY *does not see him.* HARPENDEN *goes up to him, making no sound in his stockinged feet.*)

HARPENDEN. Do I need a shave?

(MULVANEY *turns and starts when he sees the uniform.*)

MULVANEY. Gosh Almighty!

HARPENDEN. What's the matter?

MULVANEY. Is that fancy dress or are you really a gob?

HARPENDEN. I'm really a—gob. Tell me, do I need a shave?

MULVANEY (*examining his chin*). I guess it'll pass all right.

HARPENDEN (*doubtfully*). It's got to pass a lot of lynx-eyed old Admirals. (*He strokes his chin*) Damn! I think I do need a shave.

MULVANEY. Why don't you have a shave, then?

HARPENDEN. I've only got one saw-toothed old razor blade, and I can't get another.

MULVANEY. Not even for eight million dollars?

HARPENDEN (*opening the hall door and calling*). Horton. Bring my boots down, will you? (*He surveys himself critically in the mirror.*)

MULVANEY. Can you beat that—an earl being a gob.

HARPENDEN. Do you mind not using that revolting word. We say "matelot."

MULVANEY. O.K., matelot. Say, what sort of ship are you in?

HARPENDEN. Destroyer.

MULVANEY. Seen any action?

HARPENDEN. Not much. We sink the old submarine from time to time. We did have a bit of nonsense at Narvik once—a long time ago.

MULVANEY. Say, that *was* a long time ago. How long have you been in this racket?

HARPENDEN. Three years.

MULVANEY. Gosh! And they haven't made you an officer yet?

HARPENDEN. Not yet. They may this morning, though; that's what my interview at the Admiralty is about.

MULVANEY. How come you haven't been up for an interview before?

HARPENDEN. I have been—three times. This is an annual ceremony.

MULVANEY. And they turned you down—each time?

HARPENDEN. Flat, my dear Lieutenant, as a pancake.

MULVANEY. How come—you being his earlship and all that?

HARPENDEN. His earlship and all that I may be, but, as I am reluctantly forced to conclude, I am also an extremely incompetent sailor.

(HORTON *comes in with his boots.*)

HORTON. Your boots, my Lord.

HARPENDEN. Thank you, Horton.

(HARPENDEN *sits down, and* HORTON, *kneeling before him, helps him on with them.* MULVANEY *watches the scene incredulously.*)

MULVANEY. For Pete's sake!

HARPENDEN. You'd better get dressed, unless you want to receive Mabel Crum in your negligée.

MULVANEY. O.K.

(*He walks towards bedroom door, passing* HARPENDEN'S *chair as he does so, where he halts abruptly.*)

(*Mock sternly*) Isn't it customary in the British navy for a rating to stand up when an officer passes him?

(HARPENDEN, *grinning, rises smartly and stands to attention.*)

HARPENDEN. I'm very sorry, sir.

MULVANEY. So I should hope. (*He inspects him.*) All right. Carry on, my Lord. (*Chuckling*) Gee, wouldn't it slay you——

(*He goes into the bedroom.* HARPENDEN *sits down again, while* HORTON *helps him on with his other boot.*)

HORTON. High-spirited young gentlemen, these Americans.

HARPENDEN. Yes, Horton, very. By the way, you've got to look after him, after tomorrow. I'm lending him these chambers.

HORTON (*after a slight pause*). Is that wise, my Lord? You have some very breakable things here, and——

HARPENDEN. Don't worry about that, Horton. He appreciates my things much better than I do.

(*There is a ring at the front door.*)

HORTON. Very good, my Lord.

(*He goes out into the hall, and after a moment we can hear him greeting someone at the front door.*)

ELISABETH (*off*). Good morning, Horton.

HORTON (*off*). Good morning, m'lady.

(*Horton re-enters.*)

Lady Elisabeth.

(HARPENDEN *gets up, surprised.* ELISABETH *comes in.* HORTON *goes out.* ELISABETH *is very young, and seemingly quite unconscious of the fact that she is very beautiful. She is in W.A.A.F. (corporal) uniform.*)

HARPENDEN. Hullo, darling. (*He kisses her on the cheek.*) I told you—I've got to dash off to this interview in a second.

ELISABETH. I'm sorry, Bobby, but I just simply had to fly in and wish you luck.

HARPENDEN. That's very sweet of you. I need it. Well, how are you? Poor little thing. Did you have an awful journey?

ELISABETH. Awful.

HARPENDEN. Didn't you sleep at all?

ELISABETH. Not a wink.

HARPENDEN. You look very well on it, I must say. (*He points to her arm*) Hullo, haven't you gone down one? You were a sergeant last time I saw you.

ELISABETH. Yes, I know.

HARPENDEN. What's the trouble?

ELISABETH. My C.O.'s a cat.

HARPENDEN. So's my captain if it comes to that. Funny, we're neither of us awfully good at our jobs, are we?

ELISABETH. Oh, I'm quite good at mine. I just have bad luck. That's all.

HARPENDEN. What did you do this time?

ELISABETH. I lost the plans of the Station Defence.

HARPENDEN. Good Lord!

ELISABETH. Well, we found them again all right. I'd only left them in the Ladies'.

HARPENDEN. But that's nothing at all. What bad luck!

ELISABETH. You're a beast, but I love you.

HARPENDEN. Do you really?

ELISABETH. Oh, I don't know about really.

HARPENDEN. You're not beginning to have doubts on our wedding-eve?

ELISABETH. No, Bobby, it's just that it's easier for you to know about these things than it is for me.

HARPENDEN. Why, may I ask?

ELISABETH. Well, I've practically never known any other man in my life, except you—living up in that awful old Northern fastness of ours. I've always loved you, though, especially since you've been a sailor, because you look so beautiful in that uniform, with those lovely baggy trousers and that low neck——

HARPENDEN. Your view seems to be shared by their Lordships at the Admiralty.

ELISABETH. Now you—you've known hundreds of girls —thousands probably.

HARPENDEN. No, darling. Just hundreds.

ELISABETH. So it's easier for you to judge.

HARPENDEN. Judge what?

ELISABETH. Whether you love me really or not.

HARPENDEN. I love you really. (*He kisser her.*)

ELISABETH. More really than you love Mabel Crum?

HARPENDEN. Who's Mabel Crum?

ELISABETH. Darling, you know very well who Mabel Crum is. So do I, too. We hear things, you know, even up in Inverness.

HARPENDEN. I have simply no idea what you're talking about.

ELISABETH. Oh, yes, you have. (*Reproachfully*) Oh, darling, how could you?

HARPENDEN. How could I what?

ELISABETH. Mabel Crum. But she's awful.

HARPENDEN. How do you know?

ELISABETH. Why, even Daddy knows her.

HARPENDEN. I don't see why the fact that she's an acquaintance of Colonel the Duke of Ayr and Stirling should necessarily damn this lady, whoever she is.

ELISABETH. Well, you know what Daddy's like.

HARPENDEN. Darling, you shock me—really you do.

ELISABETH. Do you remember I met this Mabel Crum at a party when you were on leave, about a year ago? I pretended not to know anything about it then, because we weren't even officially engaged. But I hear now you've been seeing her again.

HARPENDEN. Your gossip, my sweet, is as untrustworthy as your father's racing tips. I haven't seen Mabel Crum for months and months. In fact, I've really no idea what can possibly have happened to her. (*He glances furtively at the door, then at his watch.*)

ELISABETH (*reproachfully*). Bobby!

HARPENDEN. What do you mean—Bobby?

ELISABETH. I always know when you're lying. You give yourself away every time.

HARPENDEN. How?

ELISABETH. I'm not going to tell you how. It's a little trick that's going to come in very useful after we're married. After we're married I shall know the exact minute when you start seeing Mabel Crum again.

HARPENDEN. Elisabeth! I consider that a perfectly revolting thing to say. Have you no moral standards of any sort?

ELISABETH (*sincerely*). I don't know. I've never had a chance of finding out.

HARPENDEN. And this is the girl I am marrying!

ELISABETH. Oh. You don't have to worry about me. It's you I'm worrying about. I have a logical mind, and I can't see why, if you see Mabel Crum before we're married, you shouldn't see her after we're married, too.

HARPENDEN. Shall I tell you why? A little bagatelle called the marriage vow.

ELISABETH. Do you mean to keep that little bagatelle?

HARPENDEN. I do.

(ELISABETH *stares at him.*)

ELISABETH. Yes, I can see you do. You're not lying now. All right, darling, I'm sorry. (*She puts her head on his shoulder*) It's only because I don't know anything about men. I've only got Daddy to go by.

HARPENDEN. For the sake of the future of the human race, I trust that that is a misleading model.

ELISABETH. He's coming round to see you this morning —on business, he says.

HARPENDEN. Oh God! Doesn't he ever do any work at the War Office?

ELISABETH. Not much. I think they only gave him the job because the army wanted to take over Dunglennon.

HARPENDEN. What is the job?

ELISABETH. Liaison Officer to the Poles.

HARPENDEN. Oh, does he speak Polish?

ELISABETH. No, but he says he understands their point of view.

HARPENDEN. I should have thought a little ready cash would have been more acceptable.

ELISABETH. Oh, he got that, too. The bookies have got it by now. Which reminds me, darling, don't put any money into Zippy Snaps, will you?

HARPENDEN. It's easy for you to sit there and say don't put any money into Zippy Snaps. Anyway, thank God, he'll miss me. I've got to go out. (*He gets up from the sofa.*)

ELISABETH. Oh, Bobby, I've just remembered. Oh, how awful! I should have told you before. There's someone else coming round to see you this morning.

HARPENDEN. Yes, darling? Who's that?

ELISABETH. Well, I haven't only asked him to come round, either.

HARPENDEN. What do you mean?

ELISABETH. I told you I had to sit up all night in the train, didn't I? Well, we were eight in the carriage, and next to me there was the most enchanting little Free French Lieutenant. Wasn't that funny?

HARPENDEN. Hilarious.

ELISABETH. Well, anyway, we talked all night, in French mostly, so the others couldn't hear what we were saying.

HARPENDEN. Darling, am I to understand that for ten

hours you regaled each other with a selection of smutty stories?

ELISABETH. No, darling, but you know what Frenchmen are. We talked of all sorts of things—his private life, my private life, General Giraud——

HARPENDEN. Darling, will you stop burbling and come to the point.

ELISABETH. Oh, yes, all right. Well, anyway, he was going up to London on leave and the poor little man had no idea where he was going to stay, so I said—— (*Noticing* HARPENDEN *start*) What's the matter?

HARPENDEN. So you said he could stay here?

ELISABETH. Yes, Bobby. I hope you don't mind, but I knew you wouldn't be using the flat after tomorrow, and I thought just for the one night you wouldn't mind him bunking in that bed with you. (*She points to bedroom door.*)

HARPENDEN. Darling, there is already a vast American bombardier bunking in that bed with me. He's in there now, dressing. I refuse pointblank, for you or for Free France, to sleep three in a bed.

ELISABETH. Oh, dear! Who's the American?

HARPENDEN. It's rather a long story to tell you now. You say this is a little Frenchman?

ELISABETH. Quite little. Of course I only saw him sitting down.

HARPENDEN. Would he fit on the sofa, do you think?

ELISABETH. Yes, I should think so.

HARPENDEN. All right. Well, you'd better stay here and explain the situation to him when he arrives. I've got to go. See you at lunch. Goodbye.

(*A thought strikes him. He looks nervously at the door.*) Or perhaps, now I come to think of it, it would be better if I just left a message for him with Horton. I mean I don't want to keep you——

ELISABETH. That's all right. I'd like to stay here. I've got nothing to do all morning.

HARPENDEN. Oh! Splendid.

(*Pause.*)

Darling, do you mind if I make a phone call?

ELISABETH. I thought you were in a hurry.

HARPENDEN. Yes, but this is something I've just thought of that's got to be done. Official business—for my Captain. (*He is dialling as he speaks. Into receiver*) Hullo, Air Ministry. Extension 5651 please . . . Hullo—Oh—this is Lord Harpenden here. Could I possibly speak to the young lady I spoke to earlier this morning . . . I forget her name . . . Oh, yes, of course, how stupid of me. (*To* ELISABETH) Terrible head for names. (*Into receiver*) Oh, hullo . . . Yes, this is Lord Harpenden. You may remember I spoke to you earlier on a certain matter. I see that you've taken no steps to expedite delivery . . . Yes, I'm glad of that . . . Well, the fact is that something has come up that renders the immediate project temporarily inoperative . . . Yes, that's exactly it . . . Exactly . . . I'll ring you later. Goodbye.

ELISABETH (*without suspicion*). What have you got to do with the Air Ministry, darling?

HARPENDEN. Oh, we work a lot with the R.A.F., you know—Coastal Command—flying boats—co-operation's all the thing these days. (*He looks at his watch*) Oh, Lord, I'm late. Goodbye, darling.

(*He kisses her. There is a ring at the front door.*)

Oh, Lord! Here's your Frenchman. You can entertain him.

(*There is the sound of voices in the hall.*)

DUKE (*off*). Good morning, Horton.

HORTON (*off*). Good morning, your Grace.

ELISABETH. No, it's not. It's Daddy.

HARPENDEN. Damn!

(HORTON *opens the door.*)

HORTON. His Grace.

(*The* DUKE *comes in. He is in Colonel's uniform, about fifty-five, rather portly, but with the remnants of great good looks.*)

DUKE. Ah, hullo, my boy. I've caught you in. Good. How are you? Looking well, anyway. All that ozone, I expect, isn't that it?

HARPENDEN. Yes, Sir. Thank you. If you'll excuse me, I must——

DUKE. That's all right, my boy; I won't keep you a second. Just wanted a little chat on certain rather pressing matters—business, you know—awful bore and all that, but it's no good shirking these things, what?

ELISABETH. Daddy—Bobby's got an interview at the Admiralty, and if he doesn't start soon he'll be late.

DUKE. What's that? Mustn't be late for the Admiralty, my boy. That'll never do.

HARPENDEN. No, sir. I quite agree.

DUKE. So I'll come straight to the point. I've just come from your solicitors. We've been looking over that marriage settlement. Well, now, that's a very handsome document, I must say—very handsome indeed. There's just one thing——

HARPENDEN. Do you mind, sir, if we discuss it some other time? If I'm late for this interview——

DUKE. Quite so, my boy, but this won't take a minute. Who's the president of your interviewing board?

HARPENDEN. I've really no idea.

DUKE. Well, find out his name and if you're late I'll give him a tinkle this afternoon and explain you were with me.

HARPENDEN. Thank you, sir. That's very kind of you, but——

DUKE. That's all right, my boy. No trouble at all. I know all these old Admirals—do anything for me, most of 'em. They're ten a penny at the Turf. Now where were we—ah yes—the settlement. Now, here's where I think it falls down. I notice that no provision whatever has been made for your wife's family.

HARPENDEN. That was agreed, sir.

DUKE. Agreed by whom? Not by me.

HARPENDEN. No, sir. You weren't consulted. By your daughter's solicitors.

DUKE. Quite so—but I must say they seem to me to have slipped up badly there. Now, there are one or two most deserving cases in our family that need attention — for instance, Elisabeth's Aunt Amy.

ELISABETH. Daddy—Aunt Amy's perfectly happy in that nursing home—and she's got plenty of money of her own——

DUKE. Quite so, my dear, but she could always do with a little more.

ELISABETH. I can't see why, seeing that she thinks she's Karl Marx.

DUKE. That hallucination is unfortunate, I know, but should not, I feel, preclude her ending her days in a manner fitting to her true estate. However, if you like, we can leave Aunt Amy out. Now—coming a little nearer home——

HARPENDEN. I made no provision for you, sir, because, as you know, I had anyway agreed to make you an allowance.

DUKE. Quite so, my boy, quite so, but these things are better on paper. On paper, my boy, signed, sealed and delivered.

HARPENDEN. I can't see why——

DUKE. My dear fellow, these days we must face facts——

ELISABETH (*sharply*). Bobby? (*She shows him her watch.*)

HARPENDEN. Oh, Lord! I'm really going to be late. Please, sir, could we face them some other time?

DUKE. I'll tell you what. I've got a car; I'll drive you round to the Admiralty, and we can talk some more about it on the way. What do you say?

HARPENDEN. Thank you, sir, only we must start now.

DUKE. Yes, yes. That's all right.

(HARPENDEN *dashes into hall. The* DUKE *gets up, has a sudden thought and goes to telephone.*)

By Jove, I nearly forgot.

ELISABETH (*frantically*). Oh, Daddy, do please hurry——

DUKE. That's all right, my dear. It'll only take a second.

ELISABETH. But Bobby's got an interview at the Admiralty.

HARPENDEN (*re-appearing*). Oh Lord, what's happened now?

DUKE.   Just a little tinkle, my boy.   I won't keep you a jiffy.

ELISABETH.   Don't worry, darling.

DUKE (*into receiver*).   Hullo—is that Macdougall and Steinbeck? . . . This is Primrose Path speaking . . . Primrose Path . . . I want fifty pounds each way . . . What's that? Oh, well, it's in the post. Yes, posted it myself . . . My dear sir, I can assure you. The old account? . . . Ah well, there was a little mistake over that. My servant forgot to post it . . . Yes, devilish stupid of him . . . My good man, I presume you know who I am? . . . Oh, you do . . . Well, really, that's nice treatment, I must say . . . Very well, then. I shall remove my custom elsewhere . . . And a very good day to you, sir. (*He rings off, furiously*) Bolsheviks! (*He begins to dial another number.*)

HARPENDEN.   Oh, God!

ELISABETH (*taking his hand. To the* DUKE) Daddy——

DUKE (*muttering*).   Damned lot of Yahoos—Macdougall and Steinbeck. (*Into telephone*) Hullo—Give me the hall porter, please . . . Hullo, Barker—this is the Duke of Ayr and Stirling . . . Will you put on half a crown each way on Bernadotte in the three-thirty for me . . . That's right. (*Impatiently*) Yes, yes, yes . . . When I see you . . .

(*He rings off. There is a ring at the front door.*)

All right, my boy. Now we can go off. Quite ready?

HARPENDEN.   Yes, sir, quite. (*He moves to the door.*)

DUKE.   Hey, wait a minute! You can't go to the Admiralty looking like a scarecrow.

(*He pulls his collar about.* HARPENDEN *gives a wail and runs to* ELISABETH.)

HARPENDEN.   Here, you fix it.

(ELISABETH *smoothes out his collar.*)

ELISABETH.   There, darling.   It looks sweet.

(HORTON *comes in.*)

HORTON.   Lieutenant Colbert.

HARPENDEN.   God in Heaven!

(COLBERT *comes in. He is a small, clean-shaven, very neat-*

looking officer in the Fighting French Forces. HARPENDEN
dashes up to him.)

Hullo. How are you? Lovely to see you. Make yourself at
home. I've got to go.

(*He disappears into the hall.* COLBERT *looks after him,
rather surprised. Then he bows to* ELISABETH.)

ELISABETH. Hullo. This is my father — Lieutenant
Colbert. Daddy, hurry up!

(*She runs out after* HARPENDEN.)

DUKE (*with an atrocious accent*). Enchanté, Monsieur,
enchanté. (*Shakes hands*) Il fait chaud aujourd'hui, n'est-
ce-pas?

COLBERT. Oui, Monsieur. Je l'ai remarqué moi-même.

DUKE. Votre figure me semble familière. Vous connaissez
Paris?

COLBERT. Oui, Monsieur, je connais Paris.

DUKE. I haven't been to Paris since the Duc de Caze
won the Grand Prix. How I used to love Paris . . . Paris
in the spring . . . The restaurants . . . the cafés . . .
the boulevards . . .

COLBERT. Et les jolies femmes, mon Colonel?

DUKE. Ah, les jolies femmes . . . I remember as a boy,
there was the most charming little thing . . .

COLBERT. Comment?

DUKE. Un charmant petit morceau . . .

(HARPENDEN *and* ELISABETH *dash in.*)

HARPENDEN. Oh, for Heaven's sake, sir!

DUKE. All right, my boy, I'm coming. (*To* COLBERT) We
must meet again, monsieur. Vous devez venir avoir un
morceau à manger avec moi, a mon club . . . Turf.

COLBERT. Avec plaisir.

DUKE. *Capitale.* (*To* ELISABETH) Goodbye, my dear. I'll
pick you up later. Now, my boy——

(*He goes out, followed by* HARPENDEN.)

HARPENDEN (*following him out*). Oh, God!

DUKE (*off, his voice coming from the hall*). The point
about this settlement, my boy, is that it's a form of
insurance——

ELISABETH. Sit down, won't you?

COLBERT. Thank you (*He sits down.*)

ELISABETH. It's all right about using this flat, except that you'll have to sleep on the sofa, just for tonight.

COLBERT. That is very kind. Who was that sailor?

ELISABETH. That was my fiancée—Bobby Harpenden.

COLBERT. Your fiancée?

ELISABETH. You're surprised?

COLBERT. You told me he was an earl. I had not expected to see him dressed in that manner.

ELISABETH. You pictured him with a little coronet and an ermine cloak?

COLBERT. Hardly, milady. But I imagined him a little older and with big moustache and a hooked nose—I do not know why.

ELISABETH. He's very good-looking, don't you think?

COLBERT. Not for me. He is altogether too—qu'est ce que c'est fâde?

ELISABETH. Insipid.

COLBERT. Yes. Too insipid.

ELISABETH. Oh.

COLBERT. I am sorry, milady, but I must say what I think.

ELISABETH. That's quite all right, only do you mind not calling me milady.

COLBERT. I beg your pardon. What must I call you, then?

ELISABETH. Well, later on last night we were calling each other Elisabeth and René.

COLBERT. Last night was—last night.

ELISABETH. And today's today. I don't see what difference . . .

COLBERT. Milady—Elisabeth—I made one of two errors last night. Either I said to you too much—or I did not say enough.

ELISABETH. Well, you didn't say too much.

COLBERT. Then I did not say enough.

ELISABETH. What more did you have to say?

COLBERT. Very much more indeed.

ELISABETH. Then say it now.

COLBERT. You would be very angry with me, if I did. No. It is better I keep silent.

ELISABETH. Very well. Just as you please.

(*Pause.* COLBERT *suddenly slaps his knee and gets up.*)

COLBERT. I shall say it. I must say it. Elisabeth—do not marry this man.

ELISABETH. Not marry Bobby? Why ever not?

COLBERT. I implore you. Turn back before it is too late.

ELISABETH. But—but I love him. Why should I——

COLBERT. You love him. Yes. You told me so last night. But you also told me what is the truth—you told me you had for him no—no passion, no white-hot burning of the heart.

ELISABETH. Oh, dear! Did I really say that?

COLBERT. You did not employ those words, but that is nevertheless what you said. You love him—oh yes, we will agree. So does one love one's brother or one's little puppy dog. But you are not *in love* with him. No, no, no, milady, Elisabeth. Not in a thousand years.

ELISABETH. But I may be in love with him. It's just that I don't know, that's all. Anyway, ordinary, quiet, restful love is a much better basis for marriage than this white-hot burning passion of the heart—or whatever you call it.

COLBERT. Oh, no, Elisabeth. Oh, no. That is where you make such a terrible mistake. Ah, I see it all so clearly. Two great English houses, the alliance planned from an age when you were both little children, obedient little children——

ELISABETH. No, no, it's not like that at all. Both of us have always been perfectly free to choose——

COLBERT. That is what your families have allowed you to believe——

ELISABETH. But—but even if I'm not in love with Bobby —and I don't admit that for a minute, mind you—but even if I'm not, at least he's in love with me.

COLBERT. Is he? And what about the woman Crum?

ELISABETH. Oh, dear! Did I tell you that?

COLBERT. Turn back, Elisabeth. Turn back, or you will ruin two lives.

ELISABETH. But this is ridiculous! What right have you to say these things to me?

COLBERT. There! I told you you would be angry.

ELISABETH. I'm not in the least angry, but the whole thing is quite absurd. Supposing I don't marry Bobby—what then? I'll go back to Inverness, and after the war I'll go on living in Dunglennon, and I'll never meet anybody again as nice or as good-looking or as—all right—as rich as Bobby; and I'll just be an old maid and sink into a decline.

COLBERT. You will not be an old maid. Nor will you sink into a decline. It is not in your face. (*He comes closer to her*) You are very beautiful, but that is nothing. You have in your eyes a joy, a desire, a voluptuous flame of life, that will not be quenched.

ELISABETH. Have I?

COLBERT. Wait, Elisabeth. Wait, and one day you will find a lover worthy of those eyes.

ELISABETH. How do you know I will?

COLBERT. I know it. That is all. You have only to wait. And I know, too, that you will not have to wait for very long.

(*There is a pause, while* ELISABETH *evidently ponders what line she ought to pursue.*)

ELISABETH. Look here, what reason have you got for saying all this to me?

COLBERT. That is a question I do not wish to answer.

ELISABETH. I believe you're making love to me.

COLBERT. You have the right to believe that, milady.

ELISABETH. I'm going to tell Bobby every single thing you've said.

COLBERT. Very well. He will strike me with a right hook, and that is unfortunate, but——

ELISABETH. I hope he does strike you with a right hook —and a left hook too——

COLBERT (*resignedly*). You see how angry I have made you. If what I said was not the truth you would not be angry; you would merely laugh.

ELISABETH. I do laugh. I think everything you've said is frightfully funny. (*Rather tearfully*) I may not be laughing outside, but I am laughing inside—like mad.

(*Pause.*)

COLBERT. I will go. (*He turns at the door*) I repeat. Turn back, Elisabeth, before it is too late. Leave this earl who does not love you to his title, his riches and his Crums.

ELISABETH. Oh, go away!

(COLBERT *goes.* ELISABETH *is plainly upset. She blows her nose violently, then goes to a big radiogram in the corner (L), opens it and switches it on. After a slight pause there comes the strains of a dance band playing a soft and sentimental air.*

MULVANEY *comes out of the bedroom, whistling cheerfully. He is dressed in American Army uniform, with wings. He stops short at sight of* ELISABETH. *He looks her up and down appraisingly, and a slow smile of satisfaction spreads across his face.*)

MULVANEY. Well, well, well. So you finally showed up?

ELISABETH (*nervously*). Hullo.

MULVANEY. I guess I'd better introduce myself. My name's Mulvaney—Lieutenant Mulvaney.

ELISABETH. How do you do. I'm——

MULVANEY (*shaking hands*). That's O.K. You don't have to tell me who you are. Your pal the earl told me all about you——

ELISABETH (*politely*). He told me about you, too.

MULVANEY. Yeah, I know. (*He stares at* ELISABETH *with undisguised admiration*) Well, well, well. I'm telling you that son of a gun didn't exaggerate one little bit. In fact, he didn't tell me the half of it. (*After another appraising stare*) Zowie!

ELISABETH (*smiling nervously*). Thank you very much.

MULVANEY. Amongst other things, he said you had a soft spot for Americans.

ELISABETH. Did he? Well, of course, I like Americans very much.

MULVANEY. Then I can see you and me are going to be friends.

ELISABETH. I hope so.

MULVANEY. Strictly between ourselves, I got a soft spot, too—for babes who look like you.

ELISABETH. That's splendid.

MULVANEY. It's terrific. Say, listen, how about a little drink? I could use one myself.

ELISABETH (*faintly*). So could I.

MULVANEY. I wonder where the earl keeps his liquor—if any.

ELISABETH (*pointing*). In that cupboard over there.

MULVANEY. Yeah. You'd know a thing like that, wouldn't you? Who better? (*He opens the cupboard*) Hot dog! There's some Scotch.

ELISABETH. Isn't there any sherry?

MULVANEY. Sherry? You wouldn't fool me, would you, Babe? You'll take Scotch and like it. (*He pours out a very large measure in a tumbler and takes it across to her, neat.*)

ELISABETH. Oh, I couldn't posibly drink that. Would you mind——

MULVANEY. Spoiling it for you? O.K.

(*He squirts a minute portion of soda water into the glass, and brings it back to her. He has poured himself another glass, neat.*)

ELISABETH. But it's much too strong.

MULVANEY. Aw, go on. It won't hurt you. (*He raises his glass*) Here's to Anglo-American relations.

ELISABETH (*after a pause, muttering*). Anglo-American relations.

(*They drink.* MULVANEY *throws his back at a gulp.* ELISABETH *takes one sip of hers and makes a wry face.*)

MULVANEY. What's the matter?

ELISABETH. It's so strong.

MULVANEY. Aw, now, you wouldn't want me to think

you a cissy, would you—in that uniform? Go on, drink it—for the honour of the R.A.F.

(ELISABETH, *obeying a sudden impulse, swallows the whole of the drink. She splutters.* MULVANEY *takes the glass from her hand and puts it down.*)
That's better.

ELISABETH (*weakly*). I'm not used to drinks as strong as that at this time in the morning.

MULVANEY (*smiling*). Yeah, yeah. I know, I know. Well, well. Now what shall we do?

ELISABETH. I don't know.

MULVANEY. You haven't any etchings to show me?

ELISABETH. Bobby has some in his bedroom.

MULVANEY. Yeah. I bet he has.

(*He laughs, as if she has made a joke.* ELISABETH *laughs too, politely, but puzzled.*)

MULVANEY. He didn't tell me you'd be in uniform. It suits you, though. Gosh, that blue brings out the colour of your eyes.

ELISABETH. Oh! Do you think so?

MULVANEY. I certainly do think so. That's one fine little pair of eyes you got yourself there, Sergeant. (*Looking at her arm*) Are you a Sergeant?

ELISABETH. No. Just a Corporal.

MULVANEY. Not for long, I'll bet. Say, aren't all the Air Marshals crazy about you?

ELISABETH. They don't appear to be.

MULVANEY. They must be a lot of blind old sourpusses. Now, if you were in the Army Air Corps——

ELISABETH. What would happen?

MULVANEY. You'd be a General.

ELISABETH. I wish I were in the Army Air Corps.

MULVANEY. You're not the only one who wishes that. Tell me, Babe, what do you like most about Americans?

ELISABETH. Well, I've met so awfully few, working where I do. But if you're typical of them, then I've got to admit that—— (*She stops.*)

MULVANEY. Go ahead. Admit what?

ELISABETH. Well—that they're a bit—different from other men.

MULVANEY. Different in a good way or a bad way?

ELISABETH (*after a slight pause*). In a good way.

(*There is a pause.* MULVANEY *jumps up.*)

MULVANEY. O.K. So let's have another drink.

ELISABETH. Oh, no—please——

(MULVANEY *has risen and is on his way to the drink.*)

MULVANEY. Say, listen—you're not fooling anyone, Babe, but yourself with this Polyanna stuff. I want another drink, you want another drink, so we both have another little drink. It's good stuff, too—pre-war, by the smell of it. (*He comes back to her with another large whisky, and one for himself*) Bottoms up, this time—or as you say—no heel taps.

ELISABETH. Oh, dear. I'd much rather not.

MULVANEY. Now, listen, if you haven't finished that drink by the time I've finished mine I'll put you over my knee and spank the life out of you.

ELISABETH. I believe you would, too.

MULVANEY. You bet your sweet life I would. Now (*he extends his glass*) here's to even closer Anglo-American relations.

ELISABETH (*muttering*). Even closer Anglo-American relations.

(*She closes her eyes and gulps it down quickly, even before* MULVANEY *has finished his.*)

(*Proudly*) There! (*She suppresses a belch*) Who's a cissy now?

MULVANEY (*admiringly*). Not you, Babe.

(*He takes her glass and puts it down.* ELISABETH *sits bolt upright on the sofa, staring straight ahead.* MULVANEY *sits beside her.*)

O.K. Shall I tell you about Bremen?

ELISABETH (*turning her head slowly, and smiling*). Oh, yes, do.

MULVANEY. Well—there we were, upside down, nothing on the clock, enemy fighters swarming all around us.

ELISABETH.   Oh, how awful!

MULVANEY.   So what did we do?

ELISABETH.   What?

MULVANEY.   Come a little closer and I'll tell you.

(ELISABETH *moves a little closer to him.*)

ELISABETH (*a trifle thickly*). What did you do?

MULVANEY.   We righted the ship, beat off the fighters, and returned to our base.

ELISABETH.   Riddled with holes?

MULVANEY.   Riddled with holes.

ELISABETH.   How wonderful!

MULVANEY.   Aw, it didn't mean a thing.

ELISABETH.   Oh, but it was. It was wonderful. Did you get the—the congresh—congrenshanell thing?

MULVANEY.   Come again?

ELISABETH (*carefully*).   The Congressional Medal of Honour.

MULVANEY.   Oh, that? No. They're thinking up something else for us, as a matter of fact.

ELISABETH.   Isn't that wonderful?

MULVANEY.   Why, it was nothing.

(*She beams at him, and then appears to be conscious for the first time of* MULVANEY'S *hand on her knee. She stares at it, more puzzled than angry.* MULVANEY *jumps up and goes to the radiogram.*)

How do you work this thing? You should know.

ELISABETH.   Oh, yes, I do. I'll show you.

(*She makes her way, a trifle unsteadily, to the radiogram and switches it on.* MULVANEY *holds out his arms to her in invitation to dance and she goes to him. They begin to sway together in unison.*)

MULVANEY.   Gosh, Baby, you're one of the loveliest things I ever saw in all my life, and I'm not kidding.

ELISABETH (*after a faint pause, looking up at him*). You're rather lovely, yourself.

(MULVANEY *hugs her closer, still in the attitude of the dance. Then he tilts her face up and kisses her. She struggles violently for a second, then succumbs and finally contributes.*

It is a long kiss. The telephone rings two or three times, unnoticed. Then MULVANEY *breaks away.*)

MULVANEY. I suppose I'd better answer that.

(*He goes to the telephone.* ELISABETH *stands in apparent ecstasy, staring straight ahead of her.*)

MULVANEY (*into receiver*). Hallo. No, he's out. Who? . . . Mabel who? . . . (*A look of horror crosses his face.*) Yeah, I'll tell him. What was the name again? . . . Yeah. That's what it sounded like . . .

(*He rings off, and stares at* ELISABETH *with horror and perplexity.*)

ELISABETH (*drowsily*). Who was that?

MULVANEY. No one. No one at all.

ELISABETH. Don't you want to go on dancing?

MULVANEY (*burbling*). Well, as a matter—I've got to rush, you know — this minute — see my Colonel — I'm late——

(*He darts out into the hall.* ELISABETH *sits down abruptly on the sofa, smiling contentedly. The* DUKE *comes in.*)

DUKE. Ah, there you are, my dear. I'm sorry I kept you waiting. I hope you haven't been bored.

ELISABETH (*drowsily*). No, Daddy. I wasn't bored. Not bored at all. Not even the teeniest little bit bored. (*She turns over on her side*) Good night, Daddy, I'm going to sleep.

(*The* DUKE, *puzzled and alarmed, approaches the sofa and looks down at his daughter, already asleep.*)

DUKE. God bless my soul! What an astonishing thing!

CURTAIN

END OF ACT I

ACT II

Scene: *The same. About 11 p.m. the same night.*

Curtain rises to disclose a man and a woman, sitting together in the same armchair. The man can be recognised as JOE MULVANEY.

HARPENDEN *enters from the hall, putting his latchkeys away in his pocket as he does so. He has his sailor's hat on the back of his head.*

HARPENDEN (*carelessly, as he passes the chair*). Hullo, Mabel.

(MULVANEY *jumps up hastily, almost spilling* MABEL CRUM *on to the floor. She is a little older than Elisabeth, but with an even wider, an even more innocent, stare of her eyes.*)

MABEL. Hullo, darling.

(HARPENDEN *gives her a peck on the cheek and makes his way to the drink cupboard.*)

MULVANEY (*embarrassed*). I didn't think you'd be back till later.

HARPENDEN. I'm sorry, Joe. I went on a pub-crawl all by myself and got bored.

(*He pours himself a whisky and soda.*)
All my friends are out of town.

MABEL. What about Freddy Dawson?

HARPENDEN. His leave's been cancelled. He went dashing back this afternoon.

MABEL. Wasn't he going to be your best man?

HARPENDEN. Yes, he was. I knew it was a mistake to choose a commando. Joe, what about you deputising for him?

MULVANEY (*uncomfortably*). Well—it's darned kind of you, Bobby—and I sure appreciate the compliment—but maybe I'd better not.

HARPENDEN. Why not?

MULVANEY. Well—I'm an American, and perhaps your family wouldn't like it.

35

HARPENDEN. I told you I haven't got any family, except a very old grandmother who can't move out of her bed and sends me an egg from time to time.

MULVANEY. It's your wife's family I meant.

HARPENDEN. They won't mind. In fact, they'd be delighted.

MULVANEY (*nervously*). No, Bobby. I don't think they'll be delighted.

HARPENDEN. Why not? It's an excellent gesture towards closer Anglo-American relations.

MULVANEY. Yeah. You're telling me. Hell, Bobby, I'd just love to do it ordinarily, and I'm sure grateful for you asking me, but count me out, there's a good guy.

HARPENDEN. Oh, all right. What about you, Mabel? I could dress you as a sailor.

MABEL. Darling, I couldn't trust myself. I'd break down and cry and tear the bride's eyes out.

HARPENDEN (*putting his arm round her waist*). Isn't she a nice girl, Joe? Don't you adore her?

MULVANEY (*without enthusiasm*). Yeah. I sure do.

MABEL. He doesn't. He thinks I'm torture.

HARPENDEN. That wasn't exactly what he appeared to be thinking when I came in.

MABEL. Darling, he was getting something out of my eye.

HARPENDEN. For a girl who takes care of her appearance, Mabel, you manage to get an inordinate amount of things in your eye.

MULVANEY. Now listen—what do you mean I think you're torture? I don't know what——

MABEL. He's fallen in love with a girl he met this morning.

MULVANEY (*alarmed*). Hey! That's not true. Whatever gave you that idea?

MABEL. He won't stop talking about how lovely she was, and how melting and soft and alluring; and then apparently he made an awful boob, because he blushes scarlet whenever he thinks of it.

MULVANEY. Hey, listen——

HARPENDEN. Who was she?

MULVANEY. Oh, no one. No one at all. I was making it all up.

MABEL. It was a W.A.A.F.

HARPENDEN. Tell us about it, Joe.

MULVANEY. Listen, Bobby. Have a heart, will you? Don't ask me about it. It's something I'm trying to forget.

MABEL. Not very hard.

HARPENDEN. He probably fell for the old confidence trick—you know—the furious father or the enraged fiancé or something.

MULVANEY. Stop it, will you. Tell us about yourself. How did the interview go? I forgot to ask you when I phoned.

(HARPENDEN *shakes his head gloomily.*)
What went wrong?

HARPENDEN. I was quarter of an hour late in the first place, then found myself overdoing the free, frank, open boyish manner, and got the jitters and became far too cringing and servile, and my hair was too long and I hadn't shaved and I didn't know how many tuppenny-halfpenny stamps I could buy for half a crown. In short, for the fourth time in this war, I proved conclusively to the Admiralty and to myself that I am not the officer type.

MULVANEY. Too bad. (*Cautiously*) Tell me. Did you see your fiancée today?

HARPENDEN. Only for a few seconds—at Brown's about drink time. I was supposed to meet her for lunch, but she rang up to say she had a headache and had gone to bed.

MULVANEY (*straightening his tie*). Headache, huh? (*Heartily*) Well, well. Do you know what I think I'm going to do? I'm going bye-byes myself.

HARPENDEN. And leave me alone with this man-eater on my wedding-eve?

MULVANEY. Aw, she's no man-eater. You don't get real man-eaters this side of the Atlantic.

HARPENDEN (*to* MABEL). If I were you, darling, I'd resent that.

MABEL. Americans always fall for the obvious. They don't appreciate subtlety.

MULVANEY. If you want to see a real man-eater you come to Elisabeth City, and I'll show you one.

HARPENDEN. Dulcie?

MULVANEY. Hell, no. Not Dulcie. I meant—Elly.

HARPENDEN. Oh, Countess Elly.

MULVANEY. Dulcie's a good girl. I'm in love with Dulcie —(*as an afterthought*) I hope.

(*He goes into the bedroom. His head appears again after a second.*)

(*Contritely, to* MABEL) Gee—Miss Crum—I must be going nuts. I forgot all about seeing you home.

MABEL. That's all right, Lieutenant. I can easily see myself home.

MULVANEY. But—hell—you live outside London—in a village called Kensington or something, don't you?

HARPENDEN. All right, Joe, don't worry, I'll see she gets home all right. You go to bed.

MULVANEY. O.K. Good night, folks.

(*He goes into bedroom.* HARPENDEN *goes to door and opens it.*)

HARPENDEN (*calling through door*). Use the side nearest the window. And don't take up all the bed, like you did last night. I spent most of the night squashed against the wall, struggling for breath.

(MULVANEY'S *head appears at the door.*)

MULVANEY. Last night I thought you were Dulcie.

HARPENDEN. Well, tonight you would oblige me by thinking I'm Hitler.

MULVANEY. O.K. Just so long as I know.

(*His head disappears.* HARPENDEN *closes the door.*)

HARPENDEN. What do you think of him?

MABEL. He's a pet.

HARPENDEN. That is a term you apply without discrimination to any member of the Allied Forces who happens to look your way. I asked you what you thought of him.

MABEL. Why so interested?

HARPENDEN. Because, if you must know, I think it's time you settled down and took to yourself a nice husband.

MABEL. Darling—not an American.

HARPENDEN. Why not?

MABEL. You don't *marry* Americans.

HARPENDEN. Don't you. Oh, well—you know best.

MABEL. Besides—what about Dulcie?

HARPENDEN. Dulcie's three thousand miles away.

MABEL (*sincerely*). Poor Dulcie.

HARPENDEN. Poor Dulcie. Did you have a good time tonight? What did you do?

MABEL. Oh, we went to the Hippodrome and had dinner at the Savoy. He was really awfully sweet. Very distrait, though. I think he really did have some rather shattering experience this morning.

HARPENDEN. Really?

MABEL. The poor pet was in such a state about it— whatever it was—that he wanted to go dashing off after dinner to the park, or somewhere, to think things out, he said.

HARPENDEN. Isn't that typically American—to go to the park to think things out?

MABEL. He didn't want to come back here at all—until I said you'd be awfully offended with him if he just faded away without saying a word. And even then he was terribly nervous and jumpy. I couldn't get him to settle down at all.

HARPENDEN. Sorry to have come barging in on you like that.

MABEL. Oh, that's quite all right, darling. Between you and me I think we were both of us delighted to see you barge in.

HARPENDEN. I'm sorry about that. Why?

MABEL. Well—he—because he doesn't like me so much and I—because I love you so much.

HARPENDEN. I bet you say that to all the sailors.

(*He kisses the top of her head.*)

MABEL. Not every sailor is as sweet as you are. And not

every sailor has two million pounds tucked away in his ditty box.

HARPENDEN. Only until nasty Mr. Gallacher takes it out of my ditty box.

MABEL. Yes, but think what fun you can have with it until he does. What fun you *have* had.

HARPENDEN. That'll be my epitaph when I swing from the lamp-post outside Albany.

MABEL. You have a morbid sense of humour, darling. (*Pause.*)

HARPENDEN. Look—it wasn't only because I was bored that I came back early tonight. I wanted to see you.

MABEL. Did you, darling?

HARPENDEN (*embarrassed*). Yes. First I thought I'd write you—then I thought that was a bit—you know—then I thought I ought to tell you—myself—although it isn't awfully easy—so——

(MABEL *looks up at him sympathetically.* HARPENDEN *turns away, in order not to meet her eyes.*)

You see, we've always been good friends and I'd hate anything—Oh God! I wish I could come to the point.

MABEL (*quietly*). You don't have to, darling. I know what the point is. After tonight you don't want to see me any more. That's it, isn't it?

(*There is a pause.*)

HARPENDEN. You're an angel.

MABEL. But—darling—don't be silly. I knew it perfectly well. I don't see you very often—you get so little leave, anyway, and when I read you were getting married I thought, well, that's that. He'll just fade quietly away and I won't ever see him again. I didn't even expect a letter—because anyway you're not a very good letter-writer, are you? I must say I'm rather grateful you told me, though.

HARPENDEN. I didn't tell you. You told me.

MABEL. You tried to, anyway. Can I get myself another drink?

HARPENDEN. Yes, of course.

(*She walks away from him to the drink cupboard and*

pours herself a drink. HARPENDEN *goes to the desk and takes an already written cheque out of the drawer. He gazes at Mabel's back in indecision, then takes her bag off the sofa, and stuffs it inside.* MABEL *turns in time to see him.*)

MABEL. What are you up to?

HARPENDEN. Nothing.

(MABEL, *drink in hand, snatches up her bag and looks inside. She takes the cheque out.*)

(*Nervously*) Just your taxi-fare home.

(*Pause, while* MABEL *examines the cheque.*)

MABEL (*at length*). My God! Darling, you *are* a bloody fool! (*She folds it up deliberately.*) The correct thing for me to do now, I suppose, is to tear it up, grind the pieces into the carpet with my heel, burst into tears and say you've insulted me.

HARPENDEN. I hope you don't.

MABEL. I won't. That's the sort of insult I appreciate. (*She gazes at it enthralled*) Those noughts make me dizzy.

HARPENDEN. Don't spend it all at once.

MABEL (*musingly*). I'll pay a quarter's rent in advance, I'll pay my dentist—he'll have a stroke—poor little man— I'll pay that swine Bojo Sprott back every cent I owe him, plus interest—I'll buy that mink coat—pay for that gin— buy that sapphire brooch and — oh, yes — I'll pay for Brenda's operation. What's left can go into war-savings. (*She puts it away in her bag.*) Darling, take that smirk off your face, and don't make any of those nasty dry comments. Will you believe me that there's never been any derrière pensée——

HARPENDEN. No, darling, arrière pensée——

MABEL. Arrière pensée, then. There's never been any thought of things like this (*she touches her bag*) behind any little—favours I may have done you in the past. My greed got the better of me just now—otherwise I *would* have torn up that cheque and made a scene. Do you believe me?

HARPENDEN. Yes, darling, I do.

MABEL. That's all—except, well—goodbye.

(*She puts her arm round his neck, and he kisses her.*)

MABEL. And thank you—very much. (*She turns quickly. Trying to laugh*) Something in my eye again.

HARPENDEN. I'll kiss it well.

(*He is going towards her when there is a ring at the front door.*)

Oh, Lord! Now who on earth's that?

MABEL. You don't suppose it's Elisabeth, do you?

HARPENDEN. I'm pretty sure not. She wouldn't come round here alone at this time of night.

MABEL. Why ever not?

HARPENDEN. She's rather — old-fashioned — in these matters.

(*There is another loud, imperious ring.*)

Horton's in bed. (*He moves towards door, then turns*) Just in case of accidents, would you mind awfully going up to the kitchen for a moment?

MABEL. Why the kitchen?

HARPENDEN. Well, it's the only other room available.

MABEL. All right, darling.

HARPENDEN. Take your drink. Have you got cigarettes?

(MABEL *nods.*)

Good. Now you go up the stairs and turn to the left—not the right, that's where Horton sleeps. (*He picks up a paper off the table*) Here's the New Statesman. (*He hands it to her*) Or would you rather I sent a man up to keep you company?

(MABEL *glances at the front page of the New Statesman.*)

MABEL. Which do *you* think?

(*She goes out. There is another loud, incessant peal of the bell.*)

HARPENDEN (*shouting*). All right. Just coming. (*He knocks on the bedroom door*) Joe! Joe! Come out of there.

MULVANEY. What's cooking?

HARPENDEN. That's exactly it. You're to go up to the kitchen, and keep Mabel Crum company.

MULVANEY. The kitchen? Why? What are we going to do up in the kitchen?

HARPENDEN. Do you need me to brief you? Here, take

a bottle of gin. (*He pushes him to the hall door*) Up the stairs and turn to the left.

(MULVANEY, *bewildered, allows himself to be pushed out into the hall.* HARPENDEN *follows him out. After a second we hear his voice in the hall.*

(*Off*) I'm very sorry, sir. I had no idea——

DUKE (*off*). That's all right, my boy.

(*The* DUKE *enters, followed by* HARPENDEN.)

I had to see you. It's most urgent. If you hadn't been in I'd have camped on your doorstep all night——

HARPENDEN (*patiently*). Yes, sir. As a matter of fact, I should have rung you up about it. I went to see my solicitors this afternoon——

DUKE (*testily*). What the dickens are you talking about?

HARPENDEN. The marriage settlement, sir. I've had them insert that clause you wanted.

DUKE. Oh, you did? Oh, well, that was good of you, my boy, extremely good of you.

HARPENDEN. Not at all, sir.

DUKE (*explosively*). Damnation!

HARPENDEN (*startled*). I beg your pardon?

DUKE. My boy, are you feeling strong enough to stand a shock?

HARPENDEN. Yes—I think so, sir—why?

DUKE. I've just come from seeing Elisabeth. I was with her for over four hours, but she's adamant, I'm afraid— adamant.

HARPENDEN. Adamant about what?

DUKE. My boy—brace yourself.

HARPENDEN. Yes, sir. I have braced myself.

DUKE. She says she's not going to marry you.

(*Pause.*)

HARPENDEN. Oh.

DUKE (*testily*). Did you hear what I said?

HARPENDEN. Yes. I heard what you said. Why isn't she going to marry me?

DUKE. That's just it. I don't know.

HARPENDEN. Oh.

DUKE. She talked a lot of gibberish about planned alliance and wrecking two lives and your not having any white-hot burning thingamagig about you—or something——

HARPENDEN. What was that about white-hot burning thingamagig?

DUKE. Well, I can't remember the words exactly—there was something about a voluptuous flame of something or other—I remember that—and then there was this white-hot poppycock and then—well, to cut a long story short, she says she's not in love with you any more.

HARPENDEN. Oh.

DUKE (*testily*). Don't keep on saying Oh.

HARPENDEN. There doesn't seem much else to say, except Oh.

DUKE. Good God, man! You're not going to let it rest at that, are you?

HARPENDEN. Well, if she feels she doesn't love me——

DUKE (*shocked*). Good Lord! I'm amazed at you, Robert, my boy. I really am. Why, if I were in your shoes, do you know what I'd do?

HARPENDEN. No. What?

DUKE. I'd raise heaven and earth to make her change her mind. I'd put up such a shindy they'd hear me in Timbuctoo.

HARPENDEN. You suggest I should stand outside Brown's Hotel and make a disturbance?

DUKE (*impatiently*). No, no, no. You misunderstand me. I mean storm her—woo her—take her by force.

HARPENDEN. That's not quite my line, I'm afraid.

DUKE. Good Lord! I thought you were a man.

HARPENDEN. What is your definition of a man, Duke?

DUKE. Someone who does something at a moment like this, instead of just standing there, wilting like a swooning lily.

HARPENDEN. Who's wilting like a swooning lily?

DUKE. You are. Why, good Lord, man, look at you——

HARPENDEN. I take it, sir, that in spite of the fact your daughter says she doesn't love me, you're still in favour of this match?

DUKE. Of course I'm in favour of this match—it's a damned good match.

(*He collects himself, goes up to* HARPENDEN *and puts his arm round his shoulders.*)

I'm fond of you, my boy—you know that. I feel about you as I'd feel about my own son.

HARPENDEN. Thank you, sir.

DUKE. Well—what are you going to do about it, eh?

HARPENDEN (*after a pause*). I'm going to have a drink. (*He goes to the drink cupboard.*)

DUKE. Robert—I'm disappointed in you.

HARPENDEN. Anything for you?

DUKE. I'll have a pint of Pommery. Got any Pommery?

HARPENDEN. No.

DUKE. Whisky and soda.

HARPENDEN. What on earth made her change her mind like this?

DUKE. Well, I've been thinking it out, and it occurred to me that something that happened this morning might have some connection——

(HARPENDEN *gives him his drink.*)

(*Automatically*) Good health. (*He drinks.*)

HARPENDEN. What happened this morning?

DUKE. Something devilish fishy. Deuced odd, the whole thing. After I'd dropped you at the Admiralty—by the way, I suppose there was no trouble about your being late, was there?

HARPENDEN. There was—but it doesn't matter.

DUKE. Sorry, my boy; I'll ring up the First Lord to-morrow. What's his name—Socialist wallah——

HARPENDEN. Alexander—but for God's sake don't. Go on. What was this fishy thing that happened?

DUKE. Well, when I came back here to pick up Elisabeth I found her in a state I can only describe as peculiar.

HARPENDEN. Peculiar? How peculiar?

DUKE. Devilish peculiar. Between you and me, my boy —and don't let it go any further—if it hadn't been Elisabeth I'd have said she was sozzled.

HARPENDEN. Sozzled? Elizabeth——

DUKE. Stinko—profundo.

HARPENDEN. I don't believe it.

DUKE. She insisted on putting her feet up on the sofa and dropping off to sleep, there and then.

HARPENDEN. Well, she had a headache. She told me so when she put me off for lunch.

DUKE (*darkly*). Yes. Later on she did have a headache. Not at the time though. She was as gay as a bee when I found her. (*In a confidential whisper*) And her breath!

HARPENDEN. Sherry?

DUKE. Whisky.

HARPENDEN. But she hates whisky.

DUKE. My boy—it was unmistakable. You can't deceive me. I've had too much experience of it in our family.

HARPENDEN. Good Lord!

DUKE. But that's not the end of it. Just before I came into the sitting-room, while I was talking to Horton out in the hall, a young man came dashing past me and out through the front door, going like the wind.

HARPENDEN. Who was it?

DUKE. Never clapped eyes on him before in all my life.

HARPENDEN. Did Elisabeth know who he was?

DUKE. Well, I asked her, and she said—and this is what makes me very suspicious—she said that he'd dropped from the skies. At first I thought she meant one of those parachutist fellows.

HARPENDEN. What did he look like?

DUKE. Well, he was tall and dark—and he was in uniform—not our uniform. As a matter of fact, I think he might have been one of those Americans who are wandering around all over London these days.

HARPENDEN. An American! Then I know who it is.

DUKE. You do? Right, my boy, your duty is plain. You must get in touch with this scallywag——

HARPENDEN. I don't need to get in touch with him. I mean, he's here.

DUKE. Here? Where?

HARPENDEN. In the kitchen.

DUKE. In the kitchen? What's he doing in the kitchen?

HARPENDEN. I tremble to think.

DUKE. Well, good Lord, don't just stand there—get him down from the kitchen.

HARPENDEN (*doubtfully*). Well, I'm not at all sure——

DUKE. Well, if you won't, I will.

(*He goes to the hall door, opens it and roars through*) Hey, you! Up in the kitchen—whoever you are. Leave whatever you're doing and come down at once! At once, do you understand? Now we'll see.

HARPENDEN. What am I to say to him?

DUKE. Leave it to me.

(MULVANEY *and* MABEL *come in together.*)

(*To* HARPENDEN) What is this woman doing here?

MABEL (*brightly, to* DUKE.) Hullo, Tibby, darling. How are you?

DUKE. Oh, it's you, Mabs.

(*He gives her a quick peck, then turns on* MULVANEY.) Now, sir, I must ask you for an explanation——

HARPENDEN (*pacifically*). By the way, this is Lieutenant Mulvaney—the Duke of Ayr and Stirling.

MULVANEY. Holy mackerel! A Duke!

DUKE. I want a straight answer to a straight question. Have you or have you not been making love to my daughter?

MULVANEY (*after a pause*). Well, here's the way it is, your —by the way, what do I call you?

DUKE. Never mind what you call me. Answer my question.

MULVANEY (*to* HARPENDEN). Is the Duke of Ayr and Whosis your father-in-law?

HARPENDEN. Yes, to be—or rather—not to be.

MABEL. Darling, what a lovely Hamlet you'd make.

DUKE. Stop it, Mabs! You shouldn't be here at all.

HARPENDEN. Darling, go back to the kitchen—do you mind?

MABEL. Oh, no. Please let me stay. This is exciting.

DUKE (*thundering*). Back to the kitchen, Mabs!

MABEL (*sulkily*). Oh, all right. (*At the door*) If the Lieutenant did make love to your daughter, you might ask her to get in touch with me sometime.

(*She goes out.* HARPENDEN *snatches up a paper and hands it to her through the door.*)

HARPENDEN. Darling, the New Statesman. (*He closes the door.*)

DUKE. Now, sir. Your answer——

MULVANEY. Well, Duke, I guess the answer is yes—I did make love to your daughter.

HARPENDEN (*hurt*). Joe!

MULVANEY. I'm sorry, Bobby. I should have told you, I guess, but I didn't have the nerve. You see, the whole thing was a ghastly mistake.

DUKE. A mistake? You have the confounded impudence to force your attentions on my daughter—after taking good care—mark you—to render her blotto—and then you stand there and tell me it was just a mistake——

MULVANEY. But it *was* a mistake, Duke. You see, I thought your daughter was Mabel Crum.

(*The* DUKE *is rendered temporarily speechless.* HARPENDEN *gives an exclamation.*)

HARPENDEN. Oh, God! Of course. I see it all now——

DUKE. You thought my daughter was Mabel Crum?

HARPENDEN. Yes, yes, of course he did. It was a perfectly natural thing for him to do.

DUKE. You will forgive me if I cannot see why it should be a perfectly natural thing for this feller to think my daughter——

HARPENDEN (*to* MULVANEY). Joe, I forgive you for everything, but whatever it was you said to Elisabeth has had the effect of making her say she won't marry me——

MULVANEY (*looking more pleased than upset*). It has? Well, can you beat that?

DUKE (*returning once more to the attack*). I may be very obtuse, but I must continue to ask why this gentleman thought my daughter was Mabel Crum.

(*There is a ring at the front door.*)

HARPENDEN. Oh, God! Joe, run and see who that is. I'm out to everybody.

MULVANEY. Sure thing.

(*He runs out into the hall.*)

DUKE. You may be satisfied with this feller's explanation, but it seems devilish flimsy to me. Why on earth should he think my daughter is Mabel Crum?

HARPENDEN Oh, for Heaven's sake, sir. He did. Isn't that enough for you?

DUKE (*roaring*). NO!

(MULVANEY *comes back.*)

MULVANEY. It's a little French guy. He says you promised him he could sleep here.

HARPENDEN. Oh, Lord! Where is he?

MULVANEY. Right here. In the hall.

(HARPENDEN *opens the door.*)

HARPENDEN. Come in, won't you?

(COLBERT *comes in.* HARPENDEN *shakes hands.*)

How are you? I'm so glad you came. Nice to see you. I wonder if you'd mind awfully going up to the kitchen for a moment?

COLBERT. The kitchen?

HARPENDEN. Yes. It's up the stairs and turn to the left. You can't miss it.

MULVANEY. It's quite comfortable up there. There are two armchairs and a bottle of gin.

HARPENDEN. And a lady who'll be absolutely delighted to see you.

(*He steers* COLBERT *towards the door and out.*)

HARPENDEN (*to* MULVANEY). Now listen. You've got to put this right, Joe.

MULVANEY. What do you want me to do, Bobby?

HARPENDEN. The best thing, I should think, would be to go round to see her at Brown's and explain the whole thing.

DUKE. What's the good of that? He'll only start making love to her again.

HARPENDEN. Oh, no, he won't.

MULVANEY (*miserably*). What makes you think I won't?

HARPENDEN. Joe!

DUKE (*triumphantly*). Did you hear that? The feller's not to be trusted an inch.

HARPENDEN (*appalled*). Joe, you're not serious?

MULVANEY. Never more serious in my life, Bobby.

HARPENDEN. But—but you've only known her since this morning.

MULVANEY. While you've known her all your life. What's the difference?

HARPENDEN. Good Lord!

(*He sinks into a chair.*)

MULVANEY. I'd never have said a word about this, if Elisabeth hadn't spoken up first.

HARPENDEN. You think she feels the same way about you?

MULVANEY. Doesn't it look that way to you?

HARPENDEN. Yes. I suppose it does. Good Lord!

(*The* DUKE, *who has been glancing from one to the other in bewilderment, now advances on* MULVANEY.)

DUKE. Am I to understand, sir, from all this rigmarole that you are now batting on an entirely different wicket?

MULVANEY (*politely*). Come again, Duke?

DUKE. A moment ago you gave as an explanation for your conduct the fact that you mistook my daughter for an unfortunate lady who shall be nameless. Now, as I understand it, you're claiming that your motives are sincere and your intentions are honourable.

MULVANEY. Well, Duke—if you want it in plain English, here it is. I think I love your daughter and I think your daughter loves me.

DUKE. Good God!

MULVANEY. Sorry, Bobby. It does seem one hell of a way to return your hospitality.

HARPENDEN (*gloomily*). For God's sake don't start apologising. I couldn't bear it.

DUKE. Oh—so you couldn't bear it. Why, good God, man, you're not going to let him snatch the girl you love from under your very nose?

HARPENDEN. How can I stop him?

DUKE. Well—good Lord—at least you can—you can fight him, can't you? Knock him for six through that window!

(HARPENDEN, sunk deep in an armchair, looks up at MULVANEY.)

HARPENDEN. He's too big. Besides, I like him.

DUKE. Like him? What's that got to do with it?

(COLBERT *comes in quietly.*)

DUKE (*testily*). Go away, Monsieur. Allez-vous-en!

COLBERT. Mademoiselle Crum has told me that something has arisen in connection with Milady Elisabeth. Might I ask, is it that Milady has decided not to marry Milord Harpenden?

HARPENDEN. Yes. That's right.

COLBERT. Then if you are searching for the reason of her decision I think I can give it to you. It is I alone who am responsible.

DUKE. What?

COLBERT. This morning I advised the Lady Elisabeth not to marry this Lord.

DUKE. Wait a minute. Am I to understand that you made love to my daughter, too, this morning?

COLBERT. I cannot deny it, Monsieur.

DUKE. But why, Monsieur? Pourquoi? I suppose because you thought she was Mistinguett?

COLBERT. No, Monsieur. Because I love her.

(*There is a moment's pause, while everyone stares at* COLBERT *wonderingly.*)

What is more, if, as you say, your daughter has taken my advice, then it appears probable that she has returned my love.

(*Another pause.* DUKE *suddenly goes to the hall door.*)

DUKE. I shall be obliged, gentlemen, if, when in due course you have concluded your deliberations, you would inform me with how many members of the United Nations my daughter is to form an attachment. Personally, I'm going up to the kitchen to have a gin with Mabel Crum.

(*He goes out. There is a pause. while* HARPENDEN *and* MULVANEY *stare, bewildered, at* COLBERT.)

COLBERT (*with quiet martyrdom*). I suppose you will wish to knock me down, Milord.

HARPENDEN. You're certainly smaller than he is—but at the moment I don't see what's to be gained by knocking you down either.

MULVANEY. Considerable satisfaction.

(*He advances belligerently on* COLBERT, *but is restrained by* HARPENDEN.)

HARPENDEN. Wait a minute, Joe. Don't start a rough-house yet. If you fight him, then I've got to fight you— and after he's recovered I've got to fight him again. Now that's too much fighting for one night. Let's try a little international arbitration first.

MULVANEY. Aw, hell, Bobby, there's no sense in arbitrating with this guy. He's screwy. He doesn't know what he's talking about. Let's you and me gang up on him and bounce him down the stairs—what do you say?

COLBERT. Tiens! I see I am facing two enemies. That is a surprise. (*To* MULVANEY) I should have thought you would have been my ally, seeing that my confession has saved you from being falsely accused of stealing this Lord's fiancée.

MULVANEY (*hotly*). Falsely accused nothing! Elisabeth is leaving Bobby because of me—see.

COLBERT. I don't think so, Monsieur. She is leaving him because of me.

(HARPENDEN *watches them with raised eyebrows*.)

MULVANEY (*belligerently*). Listen, I made love to her.

COLBERT. So did I make love to her.

MULVANEY. I said she was the loveliest thing I ever saw in all my life.

COLBERT. I, too, said she was very beautiful.

MULVANEY. Yeah—but I made real love to her—see. I kissed her.

(*Slight pause.*)

HARPENDEN (*politely*). Go on, Monsieur. Don't let it rest at that. Tell him what *you* did to my fiancée.

MULVANEY (*turning to him, contrite*). I'm terribly sorry, Bobby—but this guy's got me all balled up.

COLBERT (*to* MULVANEY). At what hour did you take these liberties with Milord's fiancée?

MULVANEY. What the hell does it matter what hour?

COLBERT. It matters very much. Try, if you will, to remember—was it after eleven o'clock?

MULVANEY. Not much after.

COLBERT. But after, none the less?

MULVANEY. Yeah. I guess so.

COLBERT. What abominable luck! Sacré nom d'une Pipe! And these attentions of yours—she repaid them?

MULVANEY. I'll say she did. (*As an afterthought*) I'm sorry, Bobby.

HARPENDEN (*ironically*). Not at all. Just imagine I'm not here. I'm going to curl up on the sofa with a good book.

(*He sits down on the sofa, picks up a book, opens it, and pretends to read.*)

COLBERT. I am also most sorry, Milord, to be forced to say such things before you.

HARPENDEN. Not at all. Don't worry about me. (*He takes his book up and then lowers it again*) Oh, before you go on—I think I ought to tell you—I hope you won't both be too angry with me—this morning I also made a little love to my fiancée; and at one moment I even went so far as to give her a kiss. I'm most terribly sorry. You must both try to be generous and forgive me.

COLBERT. At what hour was it that you gave your fiancée a kiss, Milord?

HARPENDEN. Oh yes, of course, that's very important, isn't it? It was—let me see—about ten minutes to eleven.

COLBERT. Ten minutes to eleven? That is all right, then. It was a few minutes after eleven that I advised her not to marry you and to await a lover more worthy of her.

HARPENDEN. Oh, I see. A lover more worthy of her?

COLBERT. Yes, Milord. I was naturally referring to myself and had too much delicacy to say so; but I'm afraid that it looks now as if she might have made this ludicrous error of applying my advice to this Lieutenant.

HARPENDEN (*rising*). I'm terribly sorry—you haven't been introduced, have you? Lieutenant Mulvaney—Lieutenant Colbert.

MULVANEY. Aw nuts! (*To* COLBERT) Listen, you. What right have you got to go dashing about saying those sort of things to guys' fiancées?

HARPENDEN (*from the sofa*). Ha!

MULVANEY (*to* HARPENDEN). Well, at least I had some sort of excuse for behaving as I did. He had none.

COLBERT. I have every excuse. Last night, on the train from Inverness to London, I sat next to the most adorable young girl I have yet seen in England. She is merely a Corporal W.A.A.F., so naturally I open conversation——

MULVANEY. You see the sort of guy this is—a railroad menace.

COLBERT. Not at all. When in Rome I do as the Romans, and in English trains I usually try to give the impression of having died in my seat. But this opportunity I could not let to pass. I find my W.A.A.F. is not at all what I imagine. She speaks to me in perfect French, and before long we are telling each other the most intimate details of our private lives. I find she is to marry the following day a young and immensely rich noble whom she patently—from a thousand little hints she gives me—does not love and who, it is equally patent, does not love her.

(HARPENDEN *gets up suddenly.*)

HARPENDEN (*aggressively*). And why is that so patent?

COLBERT. I find he keeps a mistress.

HARPENDEN. I keep a mistress?

COLBERT. That young woman I have just met in the kitchen—is she not a mistress?

HARPENDEN. No. She's Mabel Crum.

COLBERT. Do not misunderstand me, Milord. I am not prudish in these matters. A man can keep a hundred mistresses and still maintain a happy and successful marriage.. But when I hear that he keeps a—Mabel Crum —naturally I say—then of course he cannot love Elisabeth as wholeheartedly, as devotedly, with the same white-hot burning passion——

HARPENDEN. Aha! White-hot burning thungummy, eh?

COLBERT. Milord?

HARPENDEN. She mentioned some such idiotic phrase to her father when she told him she wasn't going to marry me.

COLBERT. She did? Splendid! Then perhaps it is still possible she has returned my passion.

MULVANEY. Listen, you little rat—the only way she'd return your passion is through the mail, marked "Not wanted."

COLBERT. The situation is not helped by impoliteness, Monsieur. We are at an impasse. You maintain she loves you, I maintain she loves me. We must devise a scheme of finding out the truth.

(HARPENDEN *goes quickly to telephone and begins to look up a number.*)

MULVANEY. Good for you, Bobby—only, say listen—let me talk to her, will you?

COLBERT. If he talks to her it is only fair play I talk to her, too.

HARPENDEN. Look, I am a patient man. I have sat— mainly in silence—while you two gentlemen have gloatingly described in the fullest and most sordid details the vile attentions you have forced on the girl I love. May I remind you, however, that you are under my roof, and you're both very much mistaken if either of you imagines that you're going to have twopence-worth of verbal loveplay with my fiancée on my telephone.

COLBERT. But—Milord—since this evening she is no longer your fiancée.

HARPENDEN. We'll see about that. (*Into receiver*) Hullo, Browns? Lady Elisabeth Randall, please . . . Yes, darling. Bobby . . . No, please don't . . . All right, then. I promise not to argue. Just tell me why—I'm surely entitled to know that . . . Yes, but your father wasn't as explicit as I'd like and . . . When will I get it? . . . Tomorrow? Yes, but I want to know tonight . . . Darling, don't cry . . . I only want to know what's happened . . . Why can't you? . . . Yes, but what's the difference between loving someone and being in love with someone . . . All right, then, tell me. Is there someone else? . . . What do you mean, you don't know? . . . Well, let me tell you, I do know——

(MULVANEY *makes a grab for the receiver, but* HARPENDEN *nudges him violently away.*)

Yes, I know more about it than you think. I know it's one of two men——

COLBERT (*urgently*). The fair play, Milord!

HARPENDEN. The fair play, my fanny! . . . Sorry, darling . . . All right, well, let me tell you—so that you'll be warned. One of them is a vicious French snake who goes about bothering young WAAFs in railway carriages, and the other is a lecherous American who mistook you for a trollop.

MULVANEY. Hey—you little rat!

(*Again he wrestles with* HARPENDEN *to grap the receiver, but is thwarted.*)

(*Shouting frantically down receiver*) Don't believe him, Elisabeth——

HARPENDEN. No, darling, I don't hear anything. Crossed line, I expect . . . Yes, darling. A trollop . . . Well, apparently he expected to find a trollop in my sitting-room . . . (*Crossly*) No, I don't know why . . . Well, you know what these Americans are, they expect to find trollops wherever they go . . . Darling, be reasonable.

(MULVANEY *gains the receiver for a moment.*)

MULVANEY (*frantically*). Don't believe him, Elisabeth— I don't think you're a trollop—I love you.

COLBERT (*grabbing the receiver from Mulvaney*). Ecoutez Elisabeth . . . I am not a vicious French snake . . . I love you passionately, devotedly, with a burning . . . She has rung off.

HARPENDEN. What did you expect?

COLBERT. Milord, I am astonished with you. Was that what you learnt on the playing-fields of Eton?

HARPENDEN. I was at Harrow.

MULVANEY (*displaying his enormous fist*). I've a good mind to punch you right in the nose.

HARPENDEN. Really! This display of righteous indignation comes a little oddly from you two gentlemen, I must say. Must I remind you that I have known and loved Elisabeth for some twenty years—while you two——

COLBERT. Palsambleu! And so what?

HARPENDEN. I beg your pardon?

COLBERT. The world is no longer what it was when this match between you and Elisabeth was first planned. Les droits de seigneur have gone—never to return. You are a doomed class.

HARPENDEN. All right. I'm a doomed class, but that's no reason I shouldn't marry the girl I love, is it?

COLBERT. Certainly it is, when that girl is Elisabeth. At all costs she must be saved from sharing your doom.

HARPENDEN. Left wing, eh?

COLBERT. Socialiste.

HARPENDEN. Well, I read the New Statesman myself.

COLBERT. That will not save you from extinction.

(MULVANEY, *who, during all this has been sunk deep in thought, makes a furtive move towards the door.* HARPENDEN *sees him.*)

HARPENDEN (*sharply*). Hey! Where do you think you're going?

MULVANEY (*a trifle shamefacedly*). Oh, I just thought I'd go out for a little stroll.

HARPENDEN. I suppose your little stroll wouldn't take you anywhere near Brown's Hotel, would it?

MULVANEY. I don't even know where Brown's Hotel is.

HARPENDEN. Then of course you wouldn't think of asking a policeman, would you?

(*He gets between* MULVANEY *and the front door.*)

HARPENDEN. No, you don't go for a little stroll. You're not leaving this flat tonight.

MULVANEY. How do you think you're going to stop me?

HARPENDEN. I don't know—but I'm going to have a good try.

COLBERT (*to* MULVANEY). If you attack Milord I shall assist him.

MULVANEY. I'm quite ready to take on the two of you.

COLBERT. Without doubt, but have you forgotten that we are guests in Milord's flat?

MULVANEY. That's no reason why he should keep me locked up in here all night like a little boy. If I want to go for a stroll, why shouldn't I go for a stroll? I'm a free man, aren't I?

HARPENDEN. If you want exercise I've got a rowing machine in the bathroom.

MULVANEY. Now, Bobby, you don't want to break the poor girl's heart, do you? She loves me, God damn it!

COLBERT. That fact is not yet fully established, Monsieur. It may well be myself she loves.

HARPENDEN. You both forget that several hours have passed since eleven o'clock this morning. All sorts of Poles, Czechs, Belgians and Dutchmen may have made love to her since then—or she may have gone dotty about the night porter at Brown's.

MULVANEY (*pleadingly*). Look, Bobby, be reasonable, will you? I got to get to see Elisabeth tonight.

COLBERT. If he goes, then I go, too.

HARPENDEN. And if you both go, I go with you.

COLBERT. Another impasse. There is only one solution.

HARPENDEN. What's that? The fair play?

COLBERT. Exactly, Milord—the fair play. Each man to go round to Brown's Hotel in turn.

MULVANEY. Yeah—but who goes first?

COLBERT (*brightly*). Alphabetical order?

MULVANEY. No, thank you, Mr. Colbert.

COLBERT. Then we must toss up a coin.

HARPENDEN. Hey, wait a minute. I don't think I agree to this.

COLBERT. Where is your spirit of sport, Milord?

HARPENDEN. Buried on the playing-fields of Harrow.

COLBERT. If you do not agree to my suggestion, Milord, then I shall be painfully compelled to side with this large Lieutenant against you. You would not then stand much chance.

MULVANEY. I got an idea. Do you guys play craps? (*He brings out some dice from his pocket.*)

COLBERT. Once—a long time ago. I have forgotten.

MULVANEY. Well, it's quite simple. Do you know how, Bobby?

HARPENDEN (*sulkily*). Yes, vaguely. You have to make seven, or something, don't you?

MULVANEY. Yeah. A seven or eleven wins straight off—two or three loses. But with anything else—say, a six or an eight—you have to throw until you make that number, when you'd win—or a seven, when you'd lose. Get the idea?

COLBERT. I think so, yes.

MULVANEY (*to* HARPENDEN). O.K., Bobby. I'll shoot you first.

(*The two men kneel down on the floor.*)
Now you take one and flip it.

HARPENDEN. Flip it?

MULVANEY. Like that (*he demonstrates*). O.K. Mine. I shoot first. (*He rolls the dice*) Eight. Now I got to roll an eight before a seven.

(*The* DUKE *comes in from the hall, unnoticed, and watches the three men.*)
(*Chanting*) Little eighter from decatur! Little eighter sweet potater! Come up. (*He throws again.*)

DUKE. I trust you are all enjoying yourselves.

COLBERT. Yes, thank you, Monsieur.

DUKE. May I ask what you're doing?

MULVANEY. Shooting craps, Duke.

DUKE (*icily*). I gather you've settled to your mutual satisfaction the unimportant little problem on which you were engaged when I left you?

HARPENDEN. Well—in a sense—this game is going to settle that.

MULVANEY (*chanting*). Come up little five and three— come up little four and four.

DUKE (*outraged*). What? Do you mean to tell me you're playing craps for my daughter?

COLBERT. We are playing to decide who proposes to her first.

DUKE (*thundering*). But this is monstrous, it's unheard of. It's—it's eighteenth-century. (*He takes a step forward*) Stop this obscenity this instant!

MULVANEY. Clear the floor, will you, Duke. You're spoiling my throw. (*He throws*) There she is. Four and four. O.K., Frenchy. Now it's you and me. Take one and flip.

DUKE (*sitting down, aghast*). Well, would you believe it? (COLBERT, *paying no attention to the* DUKE, *flips a single dice.*)

MULVANEY. O.K. That's your throw.

DUKE (*roaring*). May I remind you, gentlemen, that it's my daughter you're dicing for?

COLBERT (*throws*). Nine. Is that good?

MULVANEY. Not very. Can win, though. Try and throw another—four and five, or six and three.

COLBERT. That won't be easy. (*He throws.*)

(*The* DUKE *comes forward and watches.*)

Four. (*He throws again*) Eight. That's nearer.

MULVANEY. It's near seven, too.

COLBERT (*throws*). Ten. Suite!

DUKE. He has to throw a nine before he throws a seven, is that it?

MULVANEY. That's it, Duke.

DUKE (*thoughtfully*). You know, poor old Chicken Hartopp lost a fortune at this game at Miami.

MULVANEY. He's not the only sucker who's done that, Duke.

DUKE. I haven't played craps for years.

(*The* DUKE *kneels down to watch.* COLBERT *throws again.*)

SLOW CURTAIN

END OF ACT II

ACT III

Scene I

Scene: *The same, about 3 a.m. the following morning. The* DUKE *is engaged in throwing the dice as the curtain rises, while* HARPENDEN *is watching dourly. Both are holding glasses of whisky and soda.* COLBERT *is reclining in the armchair with his feet up on a stool.*

DUKE. Come up, little four and two. Come up for papa. (*He throws again*) There she is. There's my beauty. Six it is. (*He adds something to a much-scribbled-on score sheet, humming in high good humour*) That makes you owe me— let me see—now—five hundred and sixty-five pounds ten shillings—do you agree?

HARPENDEN (*glumly*). If you say so.

DUKE. My good child, have a look at the sheet. (*He waves it in his face.*)

HARPENDEN. That's all right. I can't add, anyway. (*He finishes his drink and gets up.*)

DUKE (*chuckling*). Can't add, my boy? No wonder they won't give you a commission. (*He finishes his drink and holds out the glass*) Here—you might get me one, too, while you're about it.

(HARPENDEN *takes his glass.*)

Now this time I think I'll put up a pony. (*He glances at the score sheet*) Twenty-five pounds. Are you on?

HARPENDEN. All right—but don't shoot till I get back.

DUKE. My dear boy—what do you think I am?

(HARPENDEN *opens his mouth to tell him, but decides against it.*)

COLBERT. Still not returned?

HARPENDEN. No. (*He consults his watch*) He's now been gone three hours and fifty minutes.

COLBERT (*unmoved*). It is nothing. Possibly she will not see him and he is still waiting in the hall of the hotel.

HARPENDEN (*gloomily*). Not Joe. He's the type who breaks down doors and things.

61

COLBERT. (*hopefully*). Then possibly he is in prison.

HARPENDEN. That's too much to hope for.

DUKE (*testily*). Don't stand there chattering. I've put a pony in the pot.

HARPENDEN (*coming back to him*). We were discussing the trivial little matter of your daughter's future, sir.

DUKE. What's that? Oh, yes. This feller's not come back yet?

(HARPENDEN *shakes his head.*)

Oh, well—I'll lay three monkeys to one against him.

HARPENDEN. I'll take that.

DUKE (*after a slight pause*). How long has he been gone?

HARPENDEN. Nearly four hours.

DUKE. Hm. Well, I'm afraid, as a father, it's hardly right for me to accept a wager like that. Sorry, old man. Now, there's twenty-five smackers in the bank, and I'm shooting. (*He rolls the dice*) Seven. Good Lord! (*Without conviction*) I hoped you were going to win that time, my boy. (*He adds the score to the sheet*) That makes you owe me six hundred pounds and ten shillings, exactly.

HARPENDEN. Just a minute. (*He snatches the sheet from him*) Five hundred and ninety pounds ten shillings.

DUKE. What's that? (*He studies the sheet*) Yes, that's right. Stupid mistake. What was that about your not being able to add?

(*The* DUKE *studies the score sheet again.* HARPENDEN *suddenly pricks up his ears at a noise outside. He darts quickly into the hall.*)

Well—Robert—I'll give you a real chance this time. I'm going to put up fifty. (*Noticing* HARPENDEN'S *absence*) Where is he?

(HARPENDEN *comes back, looking disappointed.* COLBERT *looks at him enquiringly.*)

HARPENDEN. People next door.

(COLBERT *nods and prepares to go to sleep again.*)

DUKE. I was saying, Robert, I'm going to give you a real chance this time, and——

HARPENDEN (*shortly*). Thank you, sir, but I'm not playing any more.

DUKE. But, my boy, I've won too much money off you. You'd better let me give you a few more rolls.

HARPENDEN. It's very kind of you, sir, but I'd far rather you didn't give me even one more roll.

DUKE. It's for your own good.

HARPENDEN. I am quite aware of that, sir—but I'm prepared to make that sacrifice.

DUKE. Oh, very well—if you don't want to play any more—I must say I feel very uncomfortable at winning all this money off you. That'll be—let me see now (*he studies the score sheet*)—five hundred and ninety pounds ten shillings. (*Magnanimously*) Let's wipe out the ten shillings, shall we?

HARPENDEN. No, sir. Thank you all the same.

DUKE (*stretching himself*). I feel devilish tired. Good Lord! Four o'clock—no wonder. (*Testily*) What's this damned Yankee Doodle mean by keeping my daughter out all night?

HARPENDEN. The question is not so much what does the damn Yankee Doodle mean, as what does your daughter mean.

DUKE. I'm worried. It shouldn't take her four hours to send this feller packing. (*Turning on* HARPENDEN) It's all your fault, Robert. You should never have countenanced this diabolical scheme.

HARPENDEN. No, sir.

DUKE. Why don't you ring up Brown's again instead of just standing there——

HARPENDEN. Swooning like a wilting lily?

DUKE. Exactly.

HARPENDEN. I'm not going to ring up Brown's again for the simple reason that, not ten minutes ago, when you were fully absorbed in trying to discover how you had come to cheat yourself of ten bob on the score sheet, I rang up Brown's for the fourth time since one o'clock.

DUKE (*in kindly tones*). Bit overwrought, aren't you, old man? Thought so. Know the signs well. As a matter of fact, I remember your ringing now. What did they say?

HARPENDEN. That Lady Elisabeth left shortly before twelve with an American gentleman and has not yet returned.

DUKE. Hm. Damned impertinence, isn't it? I suppose he's taken her to one of those bottle-party places, like the Jubilee or somewhere.

HARPENDEN. My own guess is Hyde Park.

DUKE (*appalled*). Hyde Park? At four o'clock in the morning? If you believe that why don't you go to Hyde Park and look for them?

HARPENDEN. How? With a torch?

DUKE. Yes, of course, with a torch.

HARPENDEN. I should be lynched, for one thing. Besides, Hyde Park is a very big place, and anyway it might be Green Park.

DUKE. Yes, or St. James's, if it comes to that, with those damned ducks. Well, there's nothing for it but to wait for this feller to come back, I suppose. I'll go and lie down on your bed for a bit, I think. All right?

HARPENDEN. All right.

DUKE (*he goes to bedroom door*). Quite sure you wouldn't care for——

HARPENDEN (*firmly*). Yes, sir. Quite sure.

DUKE (*to* COLBERT). What about you, Monsieur?

(COLBERT *raises himself on his elbow.*)

COLBERT. Pardon, Monsieur?

DUKE. Voulez vous rouler avec moi un peu?

COLBERT. Comment?

HARPENDEN. It's all right. The Duke only wants to know if you'd like to throw dice with him.

COLBERT. Ah, I see. Thank, you, Monsieur, but I never gamble, I'm afraid.

DUKE. You don't, eh? I noticed a few hours ago you had no qualms about gambling for my daughter.

COLBERT. For such a stake I would gamble all I had in the world.

DUKE. And exactly how much, if I might ask, is that?

COLBERT. In money, about twenty pounds.

DUKE. Twenty pounds. Quite so, Monsieur. (*With dignity*) I hardly think we need say any more.

(*He goes out.*)

COLBERT. He is quaint, the Duke. He is not, I imagine, typical of all your dukes?

HARPENDEN. You imagine right.

COLBERT. You do not think, by any chance, he is the Duke whom Hess came to see?

HARPENDEN. If he is, then Hess by now is almost certainly the holder of a considerable stock of Zippy-Snaps.

COLBERT. What are Zippy-Snaps?

HARPENDEN. An invention the Duke is interested in. (*He glares at Colbert malevolently*) It's an excellent scheme, as a matter of fact. Absolutely sure-fire moneymaker. You ought to put your twenty pounds into it.

COLBERT. My friend, you should not bear me a grudge. We must both acknowledge that America has conquered us.

HARPENDEN. I'm damned if I will.

COLBERT (*sighing*). They say it's a virtue in Englishmen not to know when they are beaten. In this case I would call it ridiculous bravado.

(*Pause.* HARPENDEN *continues to stride the room.*) Stop being a tiger in a cage. You make me nervous.

HARPENDEN. Good. (*He continues his walking.*)

COLBERT. Why are you in such a state? You don't really love her——

HARPENDEN. Now look. You've been saying that all the evening. If you say it once more I shall be forced to take steps.

COLBERT. What steps?

HARPENDEN. I'm wearing regulation boots. (*He displays one*) I do love her, damn it.

COLBERT. And the woman Crum?

HARPENDEN. It might interest you to know that after our marriage I'd arranged never to see the woman Crum again.

COLBERT. Tiens! As a matter of fact, it is among such women that you should choose not only your mistress but your wife.

HARPENDEN. Why, may I ask?

COLBERT. You will need a simple hard-working girl to look after you—as a mother looks after a child. But the Lady Elisabeth, it would now appear, is incapable of even looking after herself.

HARPENDEN. Why should I need looking after more than anyone else?

COLBERT. My good friend, imagine yourself when your millions are removed from you, as they will be. Look at you now—a simple sailor. Why do you think you have not yet been made an officer?

HARPENDEN. Mere class prejudice. I went to a public school.

COLBERT. In the post-war world——

HARPENDEN. Now, don't go on about my being doomed; it's beginning to depress me. Surely I'd get a pound a week from Sir William Beveridge? (*He disappears behind the curtain, emerging after a second. Hopefully*) The search-lights have suddenly come on. Perhaps the sirens will go in a minute.

COLBERT. They would not hear them. And the search-lights, crossing and inter-crossing the sky with their delicate tracery, will only make matters worse.

(*Pause.*)

HARPENDEN (*violently*). She can't do this to me, damn it!

COLBERT. My friend, she has already done it to you.

HARPENDEN. I refuse to be treated like an old sock. Why should she hurl me into the dustbin just because some rollicking American makes a pass at her? Who the hell does she think she is?

COLBERT. Ah! Now, this is more the spirit.

HARPENDEN. My God! The nerve of it! The night before our wedding! No thought for me at all. (*Imitating*) I'm not in love with you, Bobby; I love you, but I'm not in love with you. Just because she has her head filled with some idiotic, blushmaking, sentimental slush by a ridiculous little French pick-up——

COLBERT. Bravo! This is magnificent.

HARPENDEN. The utter insane selfishness of it! She knows

quite well I had to go to my Captain and beg him, on my knees—on my knees, mind you—for special leave to get married. She knows quite well—because I wrote to her—how difficult it is for me to get this leave—because of that little trouble over my last forty-eight. On my knees, I beg my Captain. "Very well, Ordinary Seaman Harpenden," he says, "I'll let you have it this time. But, my God, Ordinary Seaman Harpenden," he says, "if this is another of your damned tricks and you don't come back to me on time and married, I'll bloody well put you in irons, Ordinary Seaman Harpenden," he says. She doesn't think of me tossing and groaning and sobbing in irons, does she? Oh, no . . . Oh, dear me, no. There she is—gallivanting about the park like a Bacchante with a great big beefy brute of a bombardier, while I, her true fiancé, am left alone to face disgrace and degradation—my social life ruined, and my naval career blighted before it has begun.

COLBERT. Bravo! Bravo! It is a fine rage. Well done, Milord Bobby!

(MABEL CRUM *comes in. She looks sleepy and cross.*)

MABEL. What's all the noise about?

HARPENDEN. Good Lord! What are you doing here?

MABEL. I don't know. I thought perhaps you could tell me.

HARPENDEN. Do you mean to say you've been up in the kitchen all this time?

MABEL. I suppose I must have been. I've only just come to, to hear this extraordinary roaring coming from down here. Are you still rehearsing Hamlet, darling? Oh, God! (*She rubs her back*) I've slept in some funny places in my time, but never before in a kitchen armchair. Never again, if it comes to that.

HARPENDEN. Oh, Lord, I'm terribly sorry. I'm afraid I clean forgot about you up there. Where does it hurt? (*He massages her back.*)

MABEL. Just a little bit higher up, ducky. That's right.

HARPENDEN. Do forgive me, won't you?

MABEL. Don't be silly, darling. You've had a lot to cope with tonight, haven't you?

HARPENDEN. Rather more than usual, I admit.

MABEL. Thank you. That's all right now. (*She stretches herself*) Can I have a drink?

HARPENDEN. Yes, of course. I'll get it. (*He goes to drink table.*)

MABEL. Is Elisabeth leaving you?

HARPENDEN. Looks like it.

MABEL. For that? (*She points to* COLBERT.)

COLBERT. No, Mademoiselle. For Lieutenant Mulvaney.

MABEL. That's one better, I suppose, but she still must be cuckoo.

COLBERT. Perhaps she is not thinking in terms of pounds, shillings and pence, Mademoiselle.

MABEL (*with sincerity*). I never suggested she was. I meant she was cuckoo because the man she's turned down is ten times more attractive than the man she's turned him down for.

COLBERT. Possibly you are prejudiced, Mademoiselle——

MABEL. I'm never prejudiced about men. My God, look at him—(*she points to* HARPENDEN, *who is returning to her with her drink*)—what more could any girl want?

HARPENDEN. You just like sailors, that's your trouble.

MABEL. Of course I do. (*Taking the drink*) I'll just finish this, then I'll start my long trek home.

HARPENDEN. How are you going to get to Kensington at this time of night? We'll never get a taxi for you now.

MABEL. That's all right; I can walk.

HARPENDEN. No, of course you can't walk.

MABEL. Darling, I can't stay here, can I? So what else is there?

HARPENDEN. Yes, you can stay here. Certainly you can stay here. Why should I throw open my chambers to any odious Allied officer who likes to take a crack at pinching my girl, and then turn you, my only real friend, out into the night. You're damn well going to stay here.

MABEL. Darling, I'm not going back to that chair——

HARPENDEN. No, of course you're not. I know. You can go in Horton's bed.

MABEL. What about Horton?

HARPENDEN. Oh, I'll get him out first.

MABEL. Darling, of course. I meant, where are you going to put him?

HARPENDEN. He can go on the sofa.

COLBERT. What about myself?

HARPENDEN. H'm. Well, there's nothing else for it. You'd better go in there with me (*he points to bedroom door*). It hardly looks as if Lieutenant Mulvaney is going to honour me with his company in my bed tonight.

COLBERT. I am beginning to learn the meaning of the term "gentleman."

HARPENDEN (*to Mabel*). Just a minute. I'll get you something to sleep in. (*He opens the bedroom door. Looking inside*) His Grace, thank Heavens, is in a repulsive-looking coma.

(*He goes inside.*)

MABEL. He's terribly upset, I suppose, about Elisabeth?

COLBERT. Surprisingly so, Mademoiselle.

MABEL. Why surprisingly? He's in love with the girl.

(HARPENDEN *emerges with a pair of pyjamas over his arm. He takes them up to her.*)

HARPENDEN (*as he hands her the pyjamas*). Mabel, my dear, will you marry me?

(MABEL *gazes at him, wonderingly. Pause.*)

MABEL. Why?

HARPENDEN. Because I love you very much.

MABEL. Why else?

HARPENDEN. Because we get on well together, and I think you'd make me a very good wife.

MABEL. Yes, darling. Why else?

HARPENDEN. Because if I don't marry someone this leave I'm going to get into trouble with my Captain.

MABEL (*laughing*). Oh, Bobby, you are heaven! (*She puts her arms round his neck*) You don't really want to marry *me*. Can't you think of anyone else?

HARPENDEN. No. There isn't anyone else.

MABEL. With two million and a title you can afford the very best.

HARPENDEN. I don't wan't the very best. I want you. (*Awkwardly*) That's to say——

MABEL (*stopping his mouth*). All right, darling. Don't make it worse.

HARPENDEN. I really mean it, you know. I'm not asking you to marry me. Of course, if you'd rather not——

MABEL. Bobby, my precious, you don't think any girl in her senses would turn you down, do you?

HARPENDEN. One girl has.

MABEL. But she's not in her senses. I am. Still, before I definitely commit you, hadn't you better think hard and see if there really isn't someone you'd rather marry than me?

HARPENDEN. All right.

(*He shuts his eyes and ponders for a second.* COLBERT, *from the armchair, has been watching the scene intently.*)

(*At length*) No. There's only Lucy Scott, and she's taller than I am.

MABEL. She's an awfully nice girl, though.

HARPENDEN. Yes, but I don't think I like her awfully.

MABEL. Well, of course, if you don't like her awfully——

HARPENDEN. No, there really is only you. Do marry me.

MABEL. If I say yes, you won't try and back out, will you?

HARPENDEN. No, of course not.

MABEL. Whatever happens?

HARPENDEN. Whatever happens.

MABEL. Promise?

HARPENDEN. Promise.

MABEL. I don't want to be made what I believe is called the laughing-stock of London. All right, Bobby darling, I'll marry you.

HARPENDEN. Thanks, awfully.

(COLBERT *rises from his chair and goes up to them.*)

COLBERT. Permit me to congratulate you both.

HARPENDEN. Oh, were you there all the time? I ought to have sent you up to the kitchen.

COLBERT. I am glad you did not. I have never before attended at an English proposal. I would not have missed it for the world.

HARPENDEN (*to* MABEL). Is he being rude?

MABEL. Yes, of course he is. (*To* COLBERT, *hotly*) But let me tell you, Monsieur what's-your-name, I've been proposed to by hundreds of Frenchmen in my time, as well as all sorts of Poles, Czechs, Norwegians and the rest, and I'd far rather have an honest, straightforward English proposal like Bobby's than all that hand-kissing and arm-stroking and "Oh, but Mademoiselle is so intoxicating" stuff that you people hand out.

(*She goes out.* HARPENDEN *is about to follow her, but stops in the doorway.*)

COLBERT. In theory it should work out very well.

HARPENDEN. And in practice?

(*Pause.*)

COLBERT (*with emotion*). My dear friend, you have my very, very deepest best wishes.

HARPENDEN. Oh! (*He considers for a second.*) Well, anyway, they can't put me in irons now, can they?

(*He goes out.* COLBERT *smiles, shrugs his shoulders and goes to the telephone, where he looks up a number. He dials.*)

COLBERT (*into receiver*). Hullo. Brown's Hotel? . . . Has Lady Elisabeth come in yet? . . . Not yet? . . . No—no message.

(HORTON *comes in, looking disgruntled. He is wearing a woollen dressing-gown.*)

HORTON. Good morning, sir.

COLBERT. Good morning.

(*He goes to the sofa, and settles himself down methodically, covering himself with a rug.*)

HORTON (*at length*). Good night, sir.

COLBERT. Good night.

(*There are voices in the hall.* ELISABETH *and* MULVANEY *come in. They are looking exceedingly gay and happy.* HORTON *gets up.*)

HORTON. Good morning, my Lady.

ELISABETH. Sorry if we disturbed you.

HORTON. That is quite all right, my Lady. I realise that this is an exceptional evening. Should you want me, I shall be outside in the hall.

(*He goes out.*)

MULVANEY (*heartily*). Well, Frenchy! How you been?

COLBERT. Very well, thank you. And you?

MULVANEY. Oh, we've had a wonderful time, haven't we, Liz?

ELISABETH. Wonderful, Joe.

COLBERT. You have been in the park?

MULVANEY. Sure. How did you guess?

ELISABETH. It's the most heavenly night. There's a glorious full moon.

MULVANEY. The searchlights made a swell background.

COLBERT. I know.

MULVANEY (*to* COLBERT). Look, Buddy, do you mind fading away for a second? I got a couple of things I still want to say to Liz.

COLBERT. Very well.

(*He gazes at them for a long time, then sighs deeply, shrugs his shoulders, and goes into the bedroom.*)

MULVANEY. Well, Liz?

ELISABETH. Well, Joe?

MULVANEY. I guess this is where we say it.

ELISABETH. I guess it is.

MULVANEY. Seems kinda crazy, doesn't it?

ELISABETH. Kinda crazy is an understatement for everything that's happened to me in this last twenty-four hours.

MULVANEY. You're sure this is the way you want it?

ELISABETH. Yes, Joe, and so are you.

MULVANEY. I don't know so much about that.

ELISABETH (*smiling*). Dulcie to you.

MULVANEY. She's a good girl, Liz. Maybe one of these days I'll tell her about you.

ELISABETH. I should be careful about that. You wouldn't want to spoil Anglo-American relations, now, would you?

MULVANEY. Aw, she'd understand. She ought to be darned grateful to you, anyway, all things considered.

ELISABETH. She ought, but I wonder if she would be?

MULVANEY. Do you think Bobby should be grateful to *me*?

ELISABETH. Yes, he should. Of course he should. You've

been the little stranger that brings the severed couple together.

MULVANEY. You forget that when this little stranger appeared on the scene the couple wasn't severed anyway.

ELISABETH. Yes, we were, Joe—in a way. I wasn't sure about Bobby. I don't think he was sure about me. We'd have got married all right, but—well, with my urge to experiment, who knows what trouble there might have been later?

MULVANEY. You don't think there'll be trouble now?

ELISABETH (*smiling*). Not if you keep your promise, Joe, and go right out of my life for ever.

MULVANEY. Aw hell, Liz, I'm safe. You should know that by now. How long did we sit on that park bench?

ELISABETH. Nearly four hours.

MULVANEY. Well, in four hours did I once——

ELISABETH. No, but you did an awful lot of arguing.

MULVANEY. Arguing's nothing.

ELISABETH. That rather depends on one's opponent. No, Joe, I'm sorry. You're just a little too attractive to be what you call safe. I'll prefer you as a sentimental but distant memory.

MULVANEY. So this is where we say it?

ELISABETH. This is where we say it. Goodbye, Joe.

MULVANEY. Goodbye, Liz. (*He extends his arms.*)

ELISABETH. No, Joe.

MULVANEY. Aw, come on, Liz. You can't say goodbye for ever to a guy standing fifty feet away from him.

ELISABETH. Have you forgotten I'm getting married today?

MULVANEY. What about yesterday morning then?

ELISABETH. That was different. You thought I was a trollop.

MULVANEY. What did you think I was?

ELISABETH. One day I'll write and tell you. Now I'll just say—goodbye.

(*She kisses him.* COLBERT *appears in the bedroom door.* ELISABETH *breaks away.*)

COLBERT (*to* MULVANEY). I am most sorry to interrupt,

but the Duke is anxious to talk to you. He is in the bedroom.

MULVANEY. O.K. Don't they ever knock on doors in France?

(*He goes into bedroom.*)

ELISABETH. Is Daddy still here? I'd better see him, too.

COLBERT. Wait an instant, milady. I must say it—I shall say it. You are making a hideous, terrible mistake.

ELISABETH (*startled*). What?

COLBERT. Turn back while there is still time—turn back before you ruin yet two more lives——

ELISABETH. O, go away, you silly little man!

COLBERT. Silly little man I may be now, milady, but the day will dawn when you will see me in a different light.

(MULVANEY *appears at the bedroom door.*) What is this American to you? Nothing. No more than a single evening of voluptuousness——

MULVANEY (*advancing on* COLBERT). Oh, is that all he is?

ELISABETH. Don't pay any attention to him, Joe. Rise above him.

MULVANEY. I got a better idea. I'm going to make him rise above me. (COLBERT *quickly sits down. The* DUKE *comes in.*)

DUKE. I say, this is capital news. Capital. So you've come to your senses at last, have you, my dear? (*He kisses her affectionately.*) I never doubted it. I know you too well. Headstrong—like to kick over the traces once in a while, but no harm done. Just like your mother. There never *was* any truth in that Charley Babington story.

(HARPENDEN *comes in from the hall. The* DUKE *advances on him precipitately.*)

Ah, Robert, my boy, let me be the very first to congratulate you——

HARPENDEN (*bewildered*). Thank you, sir.

DUKE (*jovially*). You're a sly dog, Robert, I must say. How did you pull it off, eh? That's what I want to know.

HARPENDEN. Well, it wasn't awfully difficult.

ELISABETH. Just a minute, Daddy. I don't think Bobby can possibly know what you're talking about. (*To* MULVANEY) Joe—you tell him, will you?

MULVANEY. O.K. Bobby, Elisabeth has turned me down flat because she says she's now quite sure she's in love with you.

HARPENDEN. Oh.

ELISABETH. Darling, is that all you're going to say. Just —oh?

DUKE. Don't worry, old girl. That's all he ever says, whatever you tell him. Isn't that so, Robert, my boy?

HARPENDEN (*with a sickly smile*). Yes, sir.

DUKE. Go on, Robert—you old stick! Just go ahead and tell her how happy——

(MABEL *comes in, in pyjamas.*)

MABEL (*as she enters*). Darling, you always give me these awful blue pyjamas—— (*She stops at sight of* ELISABETH.)

DUKE (*outraged*). Mabs!

MABEL. Don't tell me. I know. Back to the kitchen. (*She goes out.*)

ELISABETH. That was Miss Crum, wasn't it?

DUKE (*uneasily*). Yes, dear. Little Mabs Crum—very decent sort——

ELISABETH. Oh!

DUKE. Now, you mustn't get hold of the wrong end of the stick, old girl. As a matter of fact, Mabs has been popping in and out all the evening—hasn't she, boys?

COLBERT. Yes, Monsieur.

MULVANEY. Certainly has, Duke.

ELISABETH. Oh?

DUKE (*testily*). Now, don't you start saying "Oh"! Look here, old girl, I've been in these chambers myself the whole night long. Surely that should reassure you, if nothing else, that there's been no hanky-panky——

ELISABETH. I suppose it should, but, oddly enough, it doesn't.

DUKE. But, my dear, this is a lot of ridiculous moonshine. Mabs is a sweet little child, and we're all very fond of her, but she means nothing in the world to Robert—does she, my boy?

HARPENDEN. Yes, sir—or rather no, sir—I mean——

DUKE. Well, go on, out with it. Does she or does she not?

HARPENDEN. Well, you see—the fact is, I've just asked her to marry me.

DUKE. You what?

COLBERT. It is true, Monsieur. I heard him. I even, I am afraid, encouraged the match.

DUKE (*roaring*). Will you kindly keep out of this, you interfering little jackanapes!

COLBERT (*interested*). Qu'est-ce que c'est jackanapes?

DUKE. Qu'est-ce que c'est jackanapes? C'est—c'est—tell him, someone.

HARPENDEN. Imbécile.

DUKE. You're a damned little interfering imbécile. Allez vous en! Retournez au kitchen!

(COLBERT *goes out, muttering.*)

Now, Robert, what is this all about? You must be out of your mind. You say you've asked Mabs Crum to marry you?

HARPENDEN. Yes, sir.

DUKE. But in God's name why?

HARPENDEN (*forlornly*). Well, I thought it was rather a good idea.

DUKE. A good idea? A good idea to marry Crum? A woman who's spent her whole life popping in and out of bed with every Tom, Dick and Harry——

ELISABETH. I thought you said she was such a sweet little child.

DUKE (*turning on her*). You keep out of this, too, Elisabeth. This is a matter for men to handle. Now, look here, Robert——

ELISABETH. Oh, Daddy—there's no point in going on like this. Take me home, please.

DUKE. In a minute.

ELISABETH (*shrilly*). Now! (*To* HARPENDEN) You had a perfect right to do what you like, I suppose. After all, I did turn you down.

HARPENDEN. Elisabeth, I——

ELISABETH (*turning sharply away from him*). Come on, Daddy.

DUKE (*with dignity*). All right, my dear. I'm sure I don't

want to stay another minute in the house of a raving mad-
man.

(*He goes to the door with* ELISABETH, *when a thought
strikes him, and he turns.*)

Oh, just a minute, my dear. (*He returns to* HARPENDEN)
About that money you owe me——

HARPENDEN.   What money?

DUKE.   The six hundred pounds——

HARPENDEN.   You mean the five hundred and ninety
pounds ten shillings. Yes, Duke, what about it?

DUKE.   It might interest you to know, young man, that
I intend to hand over your cheque, when you send it to me,
to charity.

HARPENDEN.   The charity in question being Messrs.
Macdougall and Steinbeck, I presume, sir?

DUKE (*after a second's speechless pause*).   No, sir. The
Society for the marrying-off of fallen women to blithering,
nancified nincompoops of earls. (*To* ELISABETH, *with
dignity*) Come, my dear.

(ELISABETH *and the* DUKE *go out.*)

MULVANEY.   I didn't make love to her, you know.

HARPENDEN (*listlessly*).   Didn't you? Why not?

MULVANEY.   She wouldn't let me.

(*Pause.*)

Congratulations on getting yourself engaged again.

HARPENDEN.   Thank you.

(*Pause.*)

(*Slowly*) I'm going to murder that bloody little Colbert.

MULVANEY.   You and me both, brother.

COLBERT *comes in from the hall, looking delighted with
himself. Both* HARPENDEN *and* MULVANEY *turn their heads
and glare at him.*)

COLBERT.   Tiens! I see I am faced by the Anglo-Saxon
bloc. (*He stretches himself and yawns*) It has been a full
night. I think, milord Bobby, I shall avail myself of your
kind invitation and stake out my claim on your bed.

MULVANEY (*to* HARPENDEN).   Is he sleeping in our bed?

HARPENDEN.   Yes, he is.

(*A thought seems simultaneously to strike them.*)

MULVANEY. Hm.

HARPENDEN. Hm.

(*They go together to bedroom door, which* MULVANEY *opens. He sweeps* COLBERT *an elaborate bow.*)

MULVANEY. After you, Monsieur.

(HARPENDEN *also makes* COLBERT *an inviting gesture towards the bedroom.* COLBERT *hesitates for some time, looking decidedly nervous. Then he straightens his shoulders with a determined air.*)

COLBERT (*murmuring*). Vive la France!

(*He walks into the bedroom with the air of an aristocrat going to the guillotine.* MULVANEY *and* HARPENDEN *follow him in and close the door.*)

CURTAIN

END OF SCENE I

SCENE II

The same, about 10 *a.m. that morning.* HORTON *enters from the hall, carrying a large tray. He deposits this on a table, knocks on the bedroom door and goes in. After a brief pause, he emerges again with the breakfast tray intact and carries it to the hall door, and out. There is a ring at the front door.*

DUKE (*off*). Good morning, Horton.

HORTON (*off*). Good morning, your Grace.

DUKE (*just in door*). Pay my taxi, will you? I've no change.

HORTON. Very good, your Grace.

(DUKE *crosses to window and then to chair.* HORTON *enters.*)

DUKE. Is nobody awake?

HORTON. All three young gentlemen were asleep when I went in just now. I shook the shoulder nearest the wall, which I took to be His Lordship's, but which proved to belong to the American gentleman. He told me to scram, which I understood to mean that they had all passed a restless night, did not wish to be disturbed, and required no breakfast.

DUKE. You've heard the news, I suppose, Horton?

HORTON. About His Lordship's engagement to Miss Crum? Yes, your Grace. He told me last night. (*Shakes his head gloomily.*)

DUKE. I agree with you, Horton. It's a shocking business. He seems absolutely set on it, I gather?

HORTON. I'm afraid so, your Grace. I did attempt to indicate my disapproval with one of my looks, but for once he seemed quite unshaken. He said it was the only way he could see to save himself from extinction in the post-war world.

DUKE. Talking like Bevin. Must be off his rocker.

HORTON. I fear so, your Grace.

DUKE. Oh, well, I suppose we must both make the best of a very bad job. Where is Miss Crum?

HORTON. In the kitchen, your Grace.

DUKE. She would be. What's she doing there?

HORTON. Having a cup of tea, I fancy, your Grace.

(MABEL *comes in, dressed.*)

MABEL. Hullo, Tibby, it was you at the door, was it?

DUKE. Yes, Mabs. Good morning. I came round specially to see you.

MABEL. Did you, Tibby? How sweet of you!

DUKE. It's not sweet of me at all. I want to talk to you seriously, on a most urgent matter.

MABEL. All right, then. Fire away.

(*She sits down. The* DUKE *sits, too. He seems awkward and embarrassed.* MABEL *takes a cigarette and the* DUKE *lights it for her.*)

Go on, Tibby. Don't keep me in suspense.

DUKE. Well, I hardly know how to begin.

(*Pause. The* DUKE *gets up and walks over to Mabel's chair.*)

(*Urgently*) Mabs—have you ever heard of Zippy-Snaps?

MABEL. Yes, of course, Tibby. Don't you remember you showed me one once? It didn't work.

DUKE. Didn't it? Astonishing thing. Faulty zipper, I suppose. Anyway, it's a wonderful invention, my dear: it'll revolutionise women's dress. None of this tiresome zipping and unzipping. Just snip snap and there you are, ready to go out. By the way (*shakes hands*), before we go any further, let me be the first to congratulate you on your engagement to young Robert.

MABEL. Oh! Did he tell you about it?

DUKE. Yes. Last night. As a matter of fact, we had a few words on the subject, I'm afraid, because at first I naturally felt a bit let down—on my daughter's behalf, you know.

MABEL. Yes, of course, Tibby.

DUKE. Still, thinking things over this morning. I thought—well—these days—it's no good crying over spilt milk, and the best thing I could do would be to come round and congratulate you both on what I am sure will be an excellent match.

MABEL. Thank you so much.

DUKE. He's a blithering young idiot, of course, in many ways, but that's beside the point. Anyway, my dear, I hope you'll both be very happy. Now—returning to Zippy-Snaps——

MABEL. Tibby, I've no money at all.

DUKE (*testily*). I know you haven't, my dear—it's not your money that we want—it's you.

MABEL (*startled*). Me?

DUKE. Exactly. Zippy-Snaps will, as we develop, cater mainly for the feminine sex, and I, as Chairman of the Board of Directors, have always maintained that what the Board needs is new blood, and—if possible—new feminine blood——

MABEL (*incredulously*). *You* want *me* on the Board of Directors?

DUKE. We do, my dear. You are exactly the sort of director—or directress, rather—that we require. A smart, young, enterprising girl, with a very well-developed business sense.

MABEL. Yes, and the fact that I'm the future Countess of Harpenden has nothing to do with it, I suppose?

DUKE. Well, of course—it's no good trying to hoodwink you, I can see—that is, I admit, a consideration. A title——

and that title especially—will look very well on the prospectus——

MABEL.   Supposing I wasn't going to marry Bobby, would you still want me?

DUKE (*soothingly*).   Of course, my dear, of course. I've told you—it's your talent and business acumen we want. (*Suspiciously*) But you *are* going to marry Bobby, aren't you?

MABEL.   Well, he's asked me to and I've said yes.

DUKE.   Capital. Well now, the whole thing is fixed. I rang up my fellow director this morning and he agreed with the project entirely. The Board, in fact, is unanimous. Well—what do you say?

MABEL.   All right, Tibby.

DUKE.   We'll get the whole thing signed, sealed and delivered, and then we'll surprise young Robert with it. My word! Won't he be proud of his little Mabs when he finds out what's happened to her. Let me see now—is there a typewriter here?

MABEL.   I don't think so. Why?

DUKE.   I thought I'd just type out a couple of letters—perfectly legal—one from me to you—the other from you to me. Then we each sign them and the thing's done. (*Goes to hall, calls off*) Horton! Horton!

(*The* DUKE *returns.*)

MABEL.   By the way, Tibby, who's your fellow director?

DUKE.   Lord Finchingfield.

MABEL.   What? Not poor old Finchy? Is he out again now?

(HORTON *comes in.*)

HORTON.   Yes, your Grace?

DUKE.   Oh, Horton, does his Lordship keep a typewriter in his chambers?

HORTON.   No, your Grace, but I do.

DUKE.   Where is it?

HCRTON.   Up in the kitchen, your Grace.

DUKE.   Lead me to it, then, Horton. Don't go away, now, Mabs, I'll be back in a jiffy.

(*He goes out.* MABEL, *left alone, goes to radiogram and switches it on. She listens to some swing music.* MULVANEY'S *head appears at the bedroom door, his eyes half-closed with sleep. He gropes his way to the radiogram, switches it off, and gropes his way back into the bedroom.*

There is a ring at the front door. MABEL *goes quickly to hall door.*)

MABEL (*off, calling*). All right, Horton, I'll answer it.

(*After a slight pause she returns with* ELISABETH.)

I thought it was you. Couldn't you get here any sooner?

ELISABETH. I came as quickly as I could. I had to finish my packing.

MABEL. I'm glad you did come, anyway. You were so rude to me on the phone I thought you wouldn't. Won't you sit down?

(ELISABETH *sits on the sofa.*)

ELISABETH. Do you mind saying what you have to say fairly quickly, as I have to catch a train at ten-forty-five?

MABEL (*looking at her watch*). I won't keep you more than five minutes. Bobby told you he'd asked me to marry him, didn't he?

ELISABETH. Yes, he did.

MABEL. Did he tell you that I'd accepted him?

ELISABETH. No, but then he hardly needed to tell me that.

MABEL. Well, I did accept him, anyway, and do you know why?

ELISABETH (*with a faint smile*). I think I can guess.

MABEL. I doubt very much if you can. Because I'm very fond of him, and because I thought I'd make him a good wife.

ELISABETH (*politely*). Really?

MABEL. He needs someone to take care of him, and I thought I'd be able to do that very well.

ELISABETH. I agree that you've never seemed to find much trouble in taking care of yourself.

MABEL. Yes. Unlike you, I had to, you see.

ELISABETH. You've managed very well.

MABEL. Thank you. I haven't done too badly for myself, I must say.

ELISABEH. To be the Countess of Harpenden is quite an achievement.

MABEL (*regretfully*). Yes, it would have been, I suppose.

ELISABETH. Why, it would have been?

MABEL. Oh, because I'm not going to go through with it. That's what I wanted to tell you.

ELISABETH. Are you serious?

MABEL. Perfectly. I told you I was very fond of him, didn't·I? That's why I can't marry him. Does that make sense?

ELISABETH. No, it doesn't.

MABEL. It does, really—if you think it out. Look, Ducky —sorry—Lady Elisabeth—you can't imagine anyone behaving as badly—from your standards—as I do, without— well, financial considerations being involved, can you? Oh, hell, this polite beating about the bush gets me down. What I'm saying is, I'm a trollop—let's face it—but not for money.

ELISABETH. What for, then?

MABEL. Men.

ELISABETH. Oh.

MABEL. Now last night, up in the kitchen, I told Bobby that if I married him I'd stay faithful to him, and I meant it. But this morning, in the cold, clear light of dawn, I just knew I couldn't go through with it.

ELISABETH. Perhaps, if you tried very hard——

MABEL. It doesn't matter how hard I tried. No—I can't lie to Bobby. So regretfully, but firmly, I've got to turn him down—which, with two million and a title involved, is really quite something, don't you agree?

ELISABETH. It *is* quite something, I do agree. I must say, I'm surprised.

MABEL. My dear, I'm amazed. But there it is. Bobby's too sweet and he's too easy to cheat. So I can't do it. Of course, with an old idiot like Tibby——

ELISABETH. You mean my father?

MABEL. Sorry, dear, I forgot he was your father. (*She looks at* ELISABETH) I must say you'd never think it. Well, there you are, Elisabeth. I'm throwing your earl back in your face. Do you still want him?

ELISABETH. I don't know.

MABEL. He still wants you.

ELISABETH. Is Bobby in there?

MABEL. All the Allies are in there.

ELISABETH. Do you think you could get him out without waking the others?

MABEL. I'll try, but it won't be easy. By the way, if you're getting married this morning, it's very unlucky to see him.

ELISABETH (*startled*). Married this morning?

MABEL. Or have you put off all the guests?

ELISABETH. No. We didn't have time. They're going to make an announcement.

MABEL. Well, that's fine. If you hurry you can still make it. It's a pity to disappoint all the guests.

ELISABETH. Yes, but—but I don't know. Well, anyway, I must see him.

MABEL. All right, then. Auntie Mabel will fix it. Now, you stand there (*she plants* ELISABETH *with her back to bedroom door*), so you can't see the door, and I'll do the rest.

(*She disappears into bedroom, emerging after a few moments with a very tousled, sleepy and disgruntled-looking* HARPENDEN, *who is walking with his eyes closed. He has on his sailor trousers and a vest.*)

HARPENDEN (*plaintively*). But why have I got to keep my eyes closed? Please, may I go back to bed? What is this?

MABEL. I'll tell you all about it in a minute. There. (*She plants him with his back to* ELISABETH.) Now, you can open your eyes.

(HARPENDEN *opens his eyes, blinking in the daylight.*)
But don't look round. Look straight ahead.

HARPENDEN. All right, I *am* looking. (*Wearily*) What's it going to be—a lovely choc. for baby?

MABEL. Yes, darling. A lovely choc. for baby. I'm not going to marry you.

HARPENDEN (*eagerly*). Aren't you? (*Discarding his obvious delight*) Aren't you, Mabel? Why?

MABEL. There really isn't time to go into that just now. Let's just say that I don't approve of marriage as an institution.

HARPENDEN.   Do you really mean you're turning me down?

MABEL.   Flat.

HARPENDEN.   Oh! I'm very upset.

MABEL.   That remark would have more conviction if you could get rid of that joyous gleam in your eye.   Goodbye. Bobby, how much do you love Elisabeth?

HARPENDEN.   Very much.

MABEL.   That's what I thought. (*She walks to the door*) Don't look round.   For the very last time in my life I am going up to your kitchen.

(*She goes out.*)

ELISABETH.   Bobby?

HARPENDEN (*without turning*).   Yes, Elisabeth?

ELISABETH.   You knew I was here?

HARPENDEN.   I guessed it.

ELISABETH.   Is that why you said you loved me very much?

HARPENDEN.   No.   That's the truth.

ELISABETH.   Do you know why we mustn't look at each other this morning?

HARPENDEN.   I guessed that, too.

ELISABETH.   Do you still want to marry me, darling?

HARPENDEN.   More than anything on earth.

ELISABETH.   In spite of everything that's happened?

HARPENDEN.   If you still want to marry me, that's good enough.

ELISABETH.   I do still want to marry you.   Much more now than ever before.

HARPENDEN.   In spite of having no white-hot burning thingummy for me?

ELISABETH.   White-hot burning thingummy is a mistake. It may be all right for some people, but not for me.

HARPENDEN.   I think I ought to warn you that I'm a doomed man.

ELISABETH.   Doomed, darling?   To what?

HARPENDEN.   Extinction, I think.

ELISABETH.   I don't mind, provided we both get extinguished together.

HARPENDEN.   That's by far the nicest thing you've ever said to me.

ELISABETH.   I can think of a nicer thing I might say.   It's true, too.

HARPENDEN.   What's that?

ELISABETH.   I'm in love with you, Bobby.

HARPENDEN.   Yes, That's even nicer.

(ELISABETH *goes to the door.*)

ELISABETH.   Don't look round.   I'll see you in five minutes' time—in church.   Goodbye.

HARPENDEN.   Goodbye.

(ELISABETH *goes out.* HARPENDEN *stands stock-still until he hears the front door bang.   Then he dashes to the bedroom door and opens it.*)

HARPENDEN (*shouting*).   Hey, you two!   Wake up!   Help me dress!   I'm getting married!

(*He dashes to the hall door.*)

(*Shouting*)   Horton, bring my boots down!   Iron my collar!   And step on it, for God's sake!

(*He dashes to bedroom door, stops, feels his chin, mutters a curse, and runs to the telephone.   He frantically looks up a number.* COLBERT *and* MULVANEY *appear at the bedroom. Both are in a state of semi-undress.*)

MULVANEY.   What's all the noise about?

HARPENDEN (*dialling*).   I'm getting married.

MULVANEY.   Yeah, I know.

HARPENDEN.   You don't know.   You can't possibly know. (*Into receiver*)   Hullo, Boots? . . .   This is Lord Harpenden —I want a new razor blade . . .   But you must have—I'm getting married! . . .   Oh, all right. . . .

(*He rings off.* HORTON *comes in.*)

HORTON.   I've had no time to iron your collar, my Lord. Is it very urgent?

HARPENDEN.   Of course it's very urgent.   I'm getting married in five minutes—hell—three minutes.   Oh, God! I suppose I can always say I'm growing a beard.

(*He darts into the bedroom.*)

HORTON.   Who is his Lordship marrying in three minutes?

MULVANEY.   Search me.

(HARPENDEN *appears at the door, struggling with his jersey.*)

HARPENDEN. Does one get married in a gas mask?

MULVANEY. It depends who you're marrying, brother.

HARPENDEN. Idiot! I meant, does one carry a gas mask —full dress, and all that? Do you know, Horton?

HORTON. I fancy not, my Lord. I am not sure if the rule applies to ratings, of course, but my brother, who is a Lieutenant Commander, did not carry his at his wedding.

HARPENDEN. All right, Horton. Jump to it, man, for heaven's sake.

MULVANEY. Hey, wait a minute. He wants to know who you're marrying, and so do we.

HARPENDEN. Oh, didn't I tell you? Elisabeth.

HORTON. I am most relieved, my Lord. You'll be leaving for Oxford after the wedding?

HARPENDEN. Yes, Horton.

HORTON. Very good, my Lord.

(*He goes out.*)

MULVANEY. Gee, Bobby, I don't know what to say.

HARPENDEN. I'll take it as said. (*They shake hands*) Thanks, Joe.

COLBERT. I, on the other hand, do know what to say. England has once again muddled through.

(*The* DUKE'S *voice can be heard in the hall.*)

HARPENDEN. Oh, God, is that old poop here? Quick, into the bedroom, both of you! If you're coming to the wedding, you've got to get dressed.

(*He pushes* COLBERT AND MULVANEY *into the bedroom, and turns as the* DUKE *and* MABEL *come in. The* DUKE *is carrying some papers.*)

Hullo, sir. See you in church.

(*He disappears into the bedroom.*)

DUKE. See me in church? Now what the dickens did he mean by that?

MABEL (*hastily*) I've no idea, Tibby.

(*She takes the papers from the* DUKE *and carries them over to the desk.*)

DUKE. See me in church? Has the boy gone off his rocker?

MABEL. Yes, ducky, I expect so. Where do I sign?

DUKE. At the bottom.

(*He points.* MABEL *quickly signs her name. As the* DUKE *sits down at the desk* HORTON, *carrying Harpenden's collar and boots, darts in from the hall, dashes across to the bedroom door and disappears inside.*)

God bless my soul! What on earth's the matter with Horton?

MABEL. Darling, I don't know. Sign that nice letter.

(*He begins to peruse the document.* HORTON *emerges from the bedroom and dashes back into the hall.*)

DUKE. Has Horton gone cuckoo, too?

(*He takes up the pen to sign.* MULVANEY, *slightly more dressed than when last seen, dashes in from the bedroom and goes to the desk, where he begins to open and close drawers violently.*)

MULVANEY. Pardon me, Duke. (*Calling*) Hey, Bobby, which drawer is that ring in?

HARPENDEN (*off*). Right-hand top.

MULVANEY (*calling*). O.K. I got it. Thanks, Duke.

(*He darts back into the bedroom, carrying a small jewel box. The* DUKE, *during* MULVANEY'S *search, has laid down his pen in disgust.*)

DUKE (*roaring*). You infernal cow-puncher. Has everyone gone raving mad in this house this morning?

(MABEL *takes up the pen and puts it into his hand.*)

MABEL. Go on, Tibby dear, I'm late for the office already.

DUKE. I've done it. (*He signs.*)

(HARPENDEN *comes in, dressed, and runs up to Mabel.*)

HARPENDEN. Darling, smooth my collar!

MABEL (*doing so*). There you are. Bobby isn't it lovely? I've just been made a director of Zippy-Snaps Incorporated.

HARPENDEN. Have you, Mabel? Aren't you a clever girl?

MABEL. I've had the most wonderful time, what with your two thousand and being made a director——

DUKE (*chuckling*). Two thousand, eh? That's a neat little engagement present, I must say.

HARPENDEN. What does he mean?

MABEL. I don't know, darling. I think he's batty, this morning. Goodbye, Bobby.

HARPENDEN. Aren't you coming?

MABEL. No. I've got to go and work.

HARPENDEN. Goodbye, then, darling. (*They kiss*) You've been an angel.

MABEL. Not really. I'd have made an awful muck of it, I know.

(*She goes to door.*)

HARPENDEN. I wish you were coming to the church.

MABEL. Better not. I might suddenly change my mind. Goodbye, Bobby dear. (*She turns to the* DUKE) Goodbye, Tibby, darling. See you on the Board.

(*She goes out.*)

DUKE. Why do you wish she were coming to the church? Why did you say you'd see me in church? What is all this church nonsense?

HARPENDEN. My God, don't you know?

DUKE. Know? Know what?

HARPENDEN. I'm marrying your daughter.

DUKE. Good God! When?

HARPENDEN (*looking at his watch*) Two minutes ago.

(*The* DUKE *stares at* HARPENDEN *for a second, then makes a dash for the hall door.*)

DUKE (*shouting, off*). Hey, Mabs! Mabs! Wait a minute! I want to see you—Mabs!

(MULVANEY *and* COLBERT *come out of bedroom, dressed.*)

MULVANEY. Say, listen, Bobby, I'm to be best man, aren't I?

COLBERT. On the contrary, he agreed that it was I who had the first claim.

MULVANEY (*hotly*). First claim! Nothing. I like that, after doing your level best to gum up the entire works.

COLBERT (*equally hotly*). I to gum up the works? Who was it who rendered the bride insensible from drink?

MULVANEY. Say, listen, there's only one way to settle

this. (*He brings out his craps from his pockets*) The fair play.

COLBERT. Very well. The fair play.

(*They kneel on the floor and each flips one dice. The* DUKE *comes back.*)

HARPENDEN. Did you catch her?

DUKE. Afraid not. She's caught *me* all right, the little scallywag.

HARPENDEN. I won't hear a word against Mabel Crum.

DUKE. Mabel Crum. What a name on a prospectus!

MULVANEY (*chanting, from the floor*). Little nine for Caroline. Five and four, hit that floor.

DUKE. Hullo! What's going on here? (*He approaches the dice players.*)

HARPENDEN. They're playing to see who's going to be best man.

DUKE. God bless my soul! What next?

MULVANEY (*chanting*). Come up for Baby! Baby wants to be best man!

COLBERT (*chanting*). This Baby wants to be best man.

DUKE. Which do you fancy—France or America?

HARPENDEN. I don't mind.

DUKE. Well, you take America then; I'll take France.

HARPENDEN. All right.

DUKE. Five hundred?

HARPENDEN. Right. Five hundred.

DUKE. Done. (*To* COLBERT) Monsieur, I've put a monkey on you.

COLBERT. Comment, Monsieur?

DUKE. J'ai metté un singe sur vous. So play up, Monsieur for the sake of the ENTENTE CORDIALE . . .

The four men are now kneeling in a row. The game proceeds to the accompaniment of chants and objurgations, and is still undecided as

THE CURTAIN FALLS

END OF PLAY.